REVISED EDITION

TROPICAL MARINE AQUARIA

BY GRAHAM F. COX
Illustrated by George Thompson

Originally published in Grosset All-Color Guide Series

GROSSET & DUNLAP
Publishers ▪ New York

The fish illustrated on our cover are found on the following pages in the book:

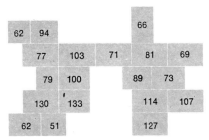

Revisions and cover photographs for the 1974 edition by Aaron Norman

REVISED EDITION

ORIGINALLY PUBLISHED IN THE
GROSSET ALL-COLOR GUIDE SERIES
1977 PRINTING

SUPERVISING EDITOR . . . GEORG ZAPPLER

2

CONTENTS

INTRODUCTION

Considering the apparently exorbitant prices of tropical marine animals (fishes and invertebrates), it is not surprising that newcomers to this absorbing hobby, and even experienced freshwater aquarists, sometimes question the advantages of setting up a tropical marine aquarium.

Then why do so? Perhaps because some of the most fascinating creatures on this planet are invertebrates, and the largest and most imposing of these can be found in salt water. Of course, some of these, such as *Daphnia*, snails, *Tubifex* worms and various aquatic insects and their larvae, can be cultured in freshwater aquaria. Usually, though, they are present as undesirable pests or as deliberately introduced live food. However, when you own a marine aquarium your horizons are limited only by the size of your tank. In your home you can witness the majestic power of a large cowrie as it 'lawnmowers' its way around the algae in your tank; the unforgettable beauty of a pink and white nudibranch mollusk as, with ballerinalike grace, it undulates through the water; the sinewy power of an octopus as it insidiously flows toward its unsuspecting prey; or the flowery form of the gently waving tentacles of a predatory anemone.

For those people who prefer their pleasures to proceed at a fast and furious pace, the relative calm of the solely invertebrate aquarium may not have much appeal. The nonstop activity and unbelievable colors of the coral-reef fishes must be enough to satisfy even this preference, however; for those who like the best of both worlds, it is possible to combine both invertebrates and fishes in the same marine aquarium.

Finally, many of the more startling discoveries recently made concerning the nature and habits of coral-reef organisms have come about as a result of the work of nonprofessional biologists carefully studying the inhabitants of their home marine aquaria. For example, what were once thought to be three distinctly different species of fishes within the wrasse family were discovered to be merely maturation color changes of the same species, the Clown Wrasse (*Coris gaimard*). Thus, intriguing prospects for study await the ambitious marine aquarist.

Maturation color changes in the Clown Wrasse

juvenile

transitional

adult

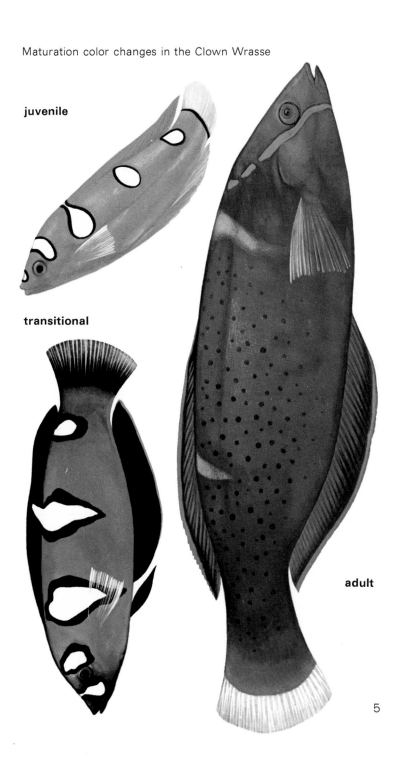

DIFFERENCES BETWEEN MARINE FISHES AND FRESHWATER FISHES

A fundamental difference between the body chemistry of seawater and freshwater fishes results from the difference in density between sea water and fresh water. Sea water has a higher specific gravity (or relative density) than fresh water because of its greater concentration of dissolved salts. In fact, the body fluids of a seawater fish have a lower salt concentration than the sea in which the fish lives. Now, as a result of the natural phenomenon known as *osmosis* (which occurs where a semipermeable membrane separates solutions of greater and lesser density), there is a tendency for water molecules to move through a fish's surface tissues from the solution of lower density to the one of higher density. In other words, a fish living in sea water will continually lose body fluids to its environmental fluid by osmosis. To counteract this loss, the marine fish has a large freshwater uptake requirement. It undoubtedly obtains some pure water from food, either directly or by chemically breaking down complex organic substances. These supplies, however, are not sufficient in themselves. Thus the sea-

By osmosis, the marine fish continually loses water to its environment. To compensate for this, pure water is obtained from sea water drunk in large quantities.

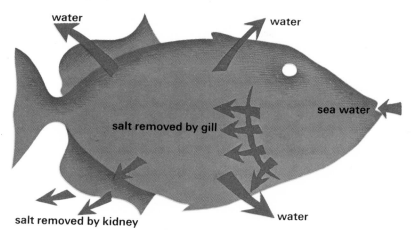

water fish continually drinks in sea water. Of course it must then extract the various salts from this water; those salts it does not need (which are in the vast majority) are excreted through special cells in the gills or as waste from its extremely efficient kidney.

If the reader has followed the explanations above, he will immediately realize that because the body fluids of the freshwater fish are *hypertonic* (stronger or more dense) in relation to its environmental fluid, the freshwater animal faces the problems of the seawater fish in reverse. By osmosis, the freshwater fish is continually taking up water through its surface tissues and is in danger of 'flooding' or 'drowning'; therefore, it must continually secrete water at a high rate.

It is always amazing to observe the metabolic versatility of the *euryhaline* fishes such as the Salmon *(Salmo salar)*, the Malayan Angel *(Monodactylus argenteus)* and the Scat *(Scatophagus argus)*, which are capable of adapting their body chemistry processes to either a marine or freshwater existence. Unfortunately, however, most of the marine fishes are *stenohaline*, in that they are unable to move freely from sea water to fresh water and back again.

Conversely, the freshwater fish gains water from its environment and must secrete it at a high rate.

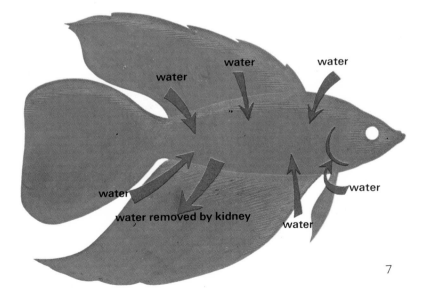

7

It will now be obvious that we are imposing an unnecesar- ily large metabolic load on marine aquarium fishes if we main- tain the water in their tank at a specific gravity that is too high. I have found with all species that the often-quoted 'normal' specific gravity reading of 1.025 should be a *maximum* level, and most fishes are happier in water of specific gravity 1.020 to 1.022 [measured at a water temperature of 75°F (24°C)].

Another difference between seawater and freshwater fishes is caused by a difference in the quality of the two types of water. In the tropics, where most freshwater aquarium fishes come from, there are large seasonal variations in water quality caused by the annual dry-season-rainy-season cycle. Periodically, and usually during the rains, relatively large amounts of organic and inorganic matter are washed into waterways inhabited by such fishes as barbs, characins, cichlids, rasboras and anabantids. These cycles of high-pollution-low-pollution have been going on for many hun-

(*Below* and *opposite*) Four species of fishes from the same area of the same reef exhibit the typical spectacular coloration of coral-reef animals.

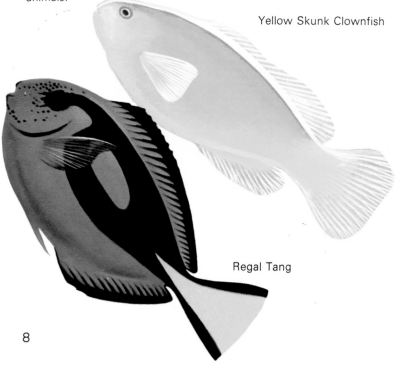

Yellow Skunk Clownfish

Regal Tang

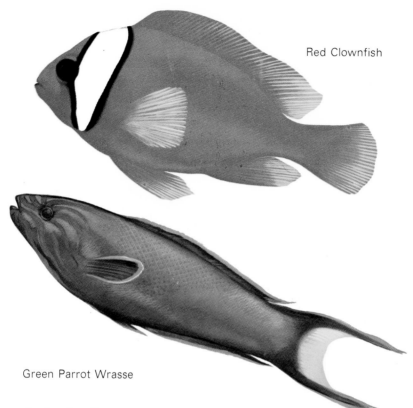

Red Clownfish

Green Parrot Wrasse

dreds of millions of years, so that the freshwater fishes have evolved compensating metabolic processes and are thus able to survive this environmental variation.

The coral reef, on the other hand, is probably the most stable habitat on this planet (after the abyssal depths, which begin 4½ miles under the surface of the sea). The changes of environmental water on the reef are so minute and slow in occurrence that the true reef-dwellers, such as the butterfly fishes (*Chaetodon* spp), have not evolved metabolic versatility to cope with sudden and drastic changes in water quality. This difference alone between seawater and freshwater fishes accounts for the puzzling experiences of many experienced freshwater aquarists; having been successful in maintaining a small (for example, 10 gallon) freshwater aquarium, they run into difficulty when attempting to maintain marine life-forms in the same tank. In such a small tank, changes in water quality

The Red Clownfish defending spawn on a rock face. Some reef fishes will spawn in aquaria but the fry do not usually survive.

that inevitably occur as the water ages more rapidly than the marine organisms can adapt. I would never recommend that anyone make a start in marine aquarium-keeping with a tank which is smaller than 20 gallons. Ideally one should obtain the largest tank permitted by the size of one's house and one's wallet.

The next difference between the two groups of fishes is one for which there is no widely accepted answer. Why are coral-reef animals so much more spectacularly colored than freshwater animals? All the fishes shown on the previous two pages come from the same area of the same reef surrounding one of the Philippine Islands, and the color variation is self-apparent. The theory that the coloration serves as camouflage would never be suggested by anyone with normal color vision who has swum on a reef. The colors make the fishes stand out like 'sore thumbs'. Perhaps the most likely explanation is the most recent one—i.e., the coloration ensures that,

A Cleaner Wrasse removing parasites from a Regal Tang. A
number of fishes on the reef provide this curious social service.

despite the enormous quantity of life on the reef and the
striking similarity in shape and size of fishes of the same
genera, members of the same species can still recognize each
other at mating times. This would prevent the catastrophe
of many matings producing sterile hybrids as a result of inter-
species crossing. Such crosses would obviously be of negative
species-survival value.

The experimentally minded marine aquarist might like to
attempt to verify or discount this hypothesis by devising
experiments which, if suitably controlled, would indicate
whether or not coral-reef fishes possess color vision. Any good
book on animal behavior and intelligence would suggest
experimental methods requiring little apparatus.

This section would not be complete without mention of
the astonishing behavior of a few fishes on the reef that
pick parasites from the bodies of other larger fishes. Such
action is an example of a *symbiotic relationship* — where both

11

partners derive benefits that assist their survival. In this case, parasites that afflict the larger fish represent a good meal to the small 'cleaner fish'. As far as I know, there is no comparable behavior among freshwater fishes.

This unusual behavior finds its most frequent expression in the attention almost incessantly paid by the small, very pretty Cleaner Wrasse (*Labroides dimidiatus* is the most common) to almost any larger fish that may be harboring parasites. However, almost all fishes of the family Chaetodontidae, the butterfly fishes and the Wimplefish *(Heniochus acuminatus)*, in particular, display this 'cleaning' behavior as juveniles. In isolated instances, 'cleaning' may even be carried through into early adulthood.

At any given temperature, the oxygen saturation of sea water is far less than that of fresh water. Thus aeration in the marine aquarium is essential to satisfy the oxygen requirements of the occupants.

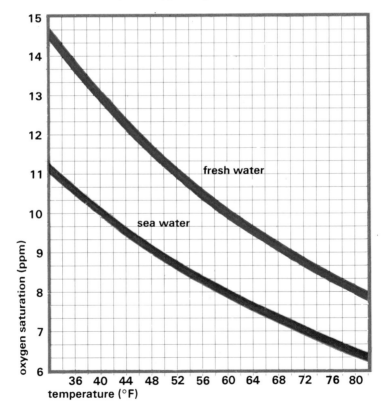

THE RIGHT CONDITIONS

Synthetic or natural sea water?
It would appear to be self-evident that any medium in which
an animal has evolved for the last few hundred million years
will be the best one to use in a life-support system for that
animal. It therefore should follow that real sea water would
be the best medium in which to culture marine organisms,
provided that it is properly cured prior to use. Unfortunately,
sea water taken straight from the sea immediately begins to
undergo many complex and not completely understood biochemical changes. Massive populations of bacteria come and
go in cycles and phytoplankton and zooplankton deteriorate
in vitality and eventually die, thus further exacerbating the
bacteria problem.

Sea water can be cured by being stored in a nontoxic
container at low temperature, between 45° and 50°F (7° to
10° C), in total darkness for four to six months. At the end of
this period the clear liquid only should be siphoned off for
use in the aquarium. This is exactly what is done at large
public marine aquaria, where big storage tanks are used for
water settling and curing. However, few nonprofessional marine aquarists can avail themselves of such facilities. Since
formulating a synthetic salt mix now sold commercially, I
have never used natural sea water in my own aquaria. During
the last few years, the results I have obtained with synthetic
sea water have been infinitely greater than those enjoyed in
my 'real sea water' days. Even long-cured natural sea water
may still contain exceptionally durable pathogens (disease-
producing organisms), whereas freshly prepared synthetic
sea water is, of course, sterile. Most better marine dealers in the
United States stock synthetic salt mixes of various brands.

Aeration
An air pump is an absolutely essential item in a marine
aquarium. The oxygen requirements of coral-reef animals
are approximately 250 percent greater than comparable freshwater animals. Their tolerance of carbon dioxide levels is
50 percent lower. In view of these requirements, it is impera-

tive that aeration and filtration systems be kept at the maximum levels 24 hours a day. Pumps must never be switched off for more than a few minutes at a time.

Filtration

Unless you are courageous enough to be considering a marine aquarium set up on the 'natural system' which will be described later, another essential item for your tank is a filter. We can differentiate between the two sorts of filtration as follows:

(1) Mechanical filtration. This term refers to the removal from the water of individually or collectively visible gross particles of detritus, uneaten food, excreta, bacteria, protozoa and so on. This type of filtration is usually sufficient to ensure water clarity. If cloudiness becomes a recurrent

The oxygen tension of foul sea water is considerably less, at a given temperature, than that of clean sea water. Filtration systems keep aquarium water clean and therefore at maximum oxygen tension.

problem, effective filtration of a second type is necessary.

(2) Biochemical filtration. This term refers to the removal from solution or the detoxification in solution of organic chemicals which could give rise to the large bacteria and plankton counts that cause persistent cloudy water.

The organic chemicals which may be present in the sea water in the aquarium are proteinaceous matter, albumenoid compounds, ionized and un-ionized ammonia and nitrite (not to be confused with nontoxic nitrate) salts. If these chemicals are present in excessive quantities, they may cause the premature deaths of all aquarium animals. Strictly speaking, nitrites and ammonia are not organic chemicals; rather, they are poisonous intermediate products in the process of bacterial breakdown of organic matter.

Highly poisonous organic matter may be introduced into the water in any one of a variety of ways as follows:

Particles in the water are trapped in a filter medium by mechanical filtration (*left*). Toxic chemicals are removed from solution or converted into harmless groups by biochemical filtration (*right*).

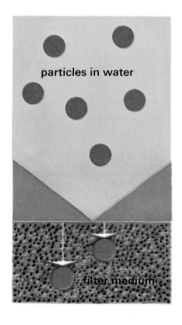 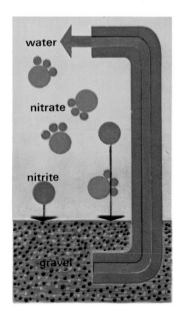

(1) by the use of uncured or inadequately cured corals or shells;

(2) by the unnoticed death and subsequent decay of an animal or plant in the aquarium;

(3) by careless overfeeding of the specimens in the marine aquarium, with the inevitable decay of uneaten food in the water;

(4) by the usage of any decorative items that release ammonia or nitrites into the water, such as calcined flint which has not been boiled for several hours prior to its introduction into the aquarium;

(5) by the addition to the water of inexpertly formulated plant-fertilizer solutions.

The whole question of filtration in the marine aquarium is fully treated later on in the book.

Specific gravity

For the nontechnical reader, a slightly more comprehensive treatment of the meaning, measurement and importance of specific gravity than has already been given will be included at this point. To begin with, specific gravity, unlike most other measurable quantities, has no units of measurement. In other words, it is correct to say that aquarium water reads specific gravity 1.021, but neither necessary nor strictly correct to say that aquarium water reads specific gravity

A hydrometer enables the aquarist to read off the specific gravity of his aquarium water

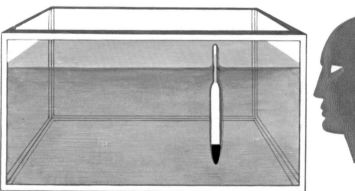

1.021 gm/cc (grams per cubic centimeter). The units are not needed since the density of pure water at 39° F (4° C) is exactly 1 gm/cc, and the specific gravity of a substance is the number of times that that substance *is heavier than an equal volume of pure water at a temperature of 39° F (4° C)*. What we are really saying therefore is that aquarium water is 1.021 times heavier than the same volume of pure water at a temperature of 39° F (4° C).

The difference in weight between sea water and the same volume of pure, fresh water is obviously caused by the salts that are present in the sea water. The more salt added, the higher the specific gravity of the solution becomes and vice versa. For high accuracy, it is necessary to relate the specific gravity reading to the temperature of the sample measured. This is because exactly the same sea water would give a lower specific gravity reading at, say, 80°F (26°C) than it would at 70°F (21°C). This will not concern the marine aquarist possessing a *hydrometer*. This is an instrument used to measure specific gravity that is calibrated for the average temperature at which marine life-forms from the tropics are normally kept.

Acidity and alkalinity

The *p*H number is another 'unitless' index number used to indicate the acidity and alkalinity of liquids. Fresh sea water usually gives a *p*H value of 8.0 to 8.3. As will be seen from the diagrammatic scale on the following page, this means that sea water in good condition is slightly alkaline. The *p*H of aquarium water is usually measured by the marine aquarist on a color scale as shown. A small amount of a chemical reagent, known as an indicator solution, is added to a measured volume of the water, and the resulting color change is compared with standard colors. This is usually sufficiently accurate for the average home aquarist's needs, although an electrically operated *p*H meter will provide greater accuracy.

Finally, it should be stated that provided the readings of specific gravity and *p*H are within the normal parameters (specific gravity 1.019 to 1.025 and *p*H 8.0 to 8.3), the actual value recorded is not nearly as important as the fact that *any changes made in these parameters should occur at the slowest possible rate.*

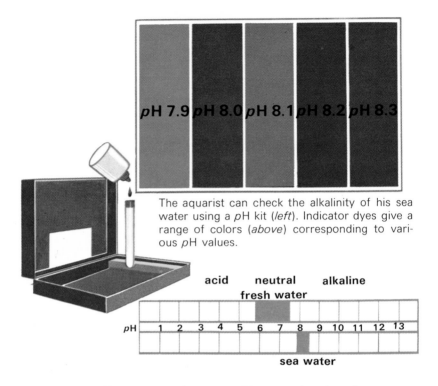

pH 7.9 | pH 8.0 | pH 8.1 | pH 8.2 | pH 8.3

The aquarist can check the alkalinity of his sea water using a pH kit (*left*). Indicator dyes give a range of colors (*above*) corresponding to various pH values.

	acid	neutral	alkaline

fresh water

| pH | 1 | 2 | 3 | 4 | 5 | 6 | 7 | 8 | 9 | 10 | 11 | 12 | 13 |

sea water

The pH of fresh water varies over a wider range than that of sea water. Fresh water is slightly acid, sea water slightly alkaline. (pH 7 = neutral).

Lighting

The amount of lighting necessary to illuminate a marine aquarium is an open question. A few aquarists may wish to maintain the decorative items in the aquarium, for example corals, shells and rocks, in a state of virgin cleanliness; if so, they will be advised to keep the illumination to the lowest level that permits easy viewing of the aquarium's occupants. The reason for this is that in either natural sea water or well-formulated synthetic sea water there are salts present such as nitrates and phosphates, along with traces of certain metals (potassium, boron, iron, magnesium and others) and nonmetals (sulphur and iodine) that are vital nutrients stimulating plant growth. With lighting at a high intensity, approaching that of light falling on the reef, all decorative items within the aquarium quickly become coated with a patina of delicately shaded green and brown algae.

Most aquarists, however, feel that algae is desirable. To get a rich, natural covering of algae, it is almost impossible to have too much light in a marine aquarium. There are limiting factors, however. Overheating of the aquarium water will cause the oxygen tension to fall drastically, which can immediately kill the fishes; furthermore, high electricity bills, though less immediate and dramatic, can be equally disturbing.

Most readers will know that white light is actually made up of red, orange, yellow, green, blue, indigo and violet mixed together. What many may not know is that these component wave lengths have varying abilities to penetrate water. In fact, the light from the red end of the spectrum has less ability to penetrate sea water than light from the blue end.

It so happens that green plants require more red than blue light, whereas brown and red algae need more blue-green light than red.

Fluorescent light has a greater blue than red content (*left*) while incandescent light has a greater red than blue content (*right*).

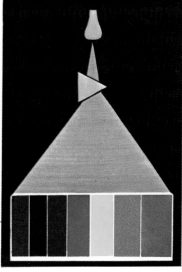

Obviously then, in choosing the correct lighting for the job, we must examine the different qualities of light emitted from available light sources. Generally, incandescent (tungsten or carbon filament) bulbs emit light with a greater red content than the normal fluorescent tube, although color-corrected fluorescent tubes are available that go a long way toward adjusting this chromatic imbalance. An advantage of fluorescent tubes over incandescent light sources is that in the former, almost all the electricity used is converted into light, whereas in the latter a good proportion of it is wasted as heat. Conversely, the initial cost of a fluorescent tube and the control equipment needed to run it is high, whereas a light bulb and holder cost little.

There are two compromise solutions to this problem:
(1) an incandescent striplight and a normal white fluorescent tube;
(2) a color-corrected fluorescent tube and a normal white fluorescent tube.

Both, of course, should be fitted in a correctly designed hood as shown.

The aquarium hood should carry the light source at the front of the tank (*below*), so that the occupants are viewed by reflected light. Transmitted light from the rear of the tank (*bottom*) will affect the colors of the fishes.

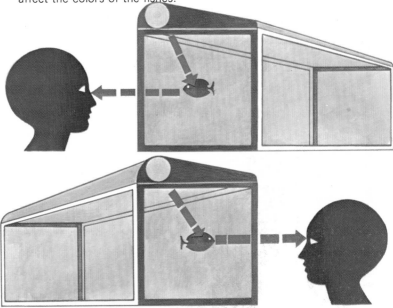

THE RIGHT EQUIPMENT

Choosing the tank

Basically, an aquarium is a strong container that allows us to view its contents and therefore enjoy our miniature coral reef at home. Unfortunately, there are so many variations on the apparently simple 'strong container' theme that we must first examine the special qualities that the marine aquarist should expect of his tank, and then rank the available types in order of increasing suitability for our purposes.

Sea water, whether natural or synthetic, is extremely corrosive. It contains many chemicals that readily attack metals, including most stainless steels. It is obvious, then, that if any type of metal-framed tank is used, the frame must be protected from contact with the water by some insulating layer of inert material. In the early days the only way a pioneer marine aquarist could obtain effective protection was to paint the angle-iron frame of the tank very carefully. This is still the cheapest way of preparing a marine aquarium, provided that care is taken when the tank is in use

A metal-framed glass tank can be used as a marine aquarium provided the angle-iron framework is painted and all the internal seams are sealed.

to ensure that this vital layer of paint is not scratched, as this would expose the underlying steel to attacks of rust. This will be of interest to the established freshwater aquarist who may be considering converting one of his old tanks for use as a marine aquarium. It is strongly recommended that in addition to carrying out top-quality paintwork on the frame, such a conversion should also include the sealing of all internal seams of the aquarium with an approved silicone sealant. This is necessary for any conventional putty-glazed tank, because many glazing compounds used are toxic to marine animals. In any event, treating a tank in this way renders it permanently leakproof, even many years later when the putty has dried, cracked and lost its adhesive qualities. Even if such a tank should rust, the effect of corrosion is unlikely to kill the fishes.

Other variations of protected metal-framed tanks are the nylon-coated iron-framed tank, the polyester- or epoxy-coated iron-framed tank and, more recently, the anodized-aluminum-framed tank. In the last example, serious aluminum poisoning of the water will result if the anodized surface is scratched on any part of the top frame that is in contact with the water.

All-glass tanks, which have come into being thanks to the

Alternatively, the metal frame can be protected by a nylon or plastic coat.

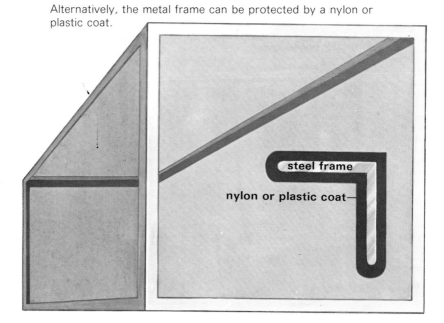

steel frame

nylon or plastic coat—

silicone-rubber adhesive sealants mentioned above, work well. Sheets of glass are simply glued together to make this surprisingly strong, nontoxic, noncorrodible container, which can be made or purchased at reasonable cost.

Next in order of suitability are all-plastic aquaria. These are usually made of acrylic plastics. Small tanks up to 36 inches x 12 inches x 12 inches are mass-produced by vacuum-forming. Larger units are fabricated from plastic sheets. Their advantages are low weight and, in the case of the small mass-produced units, low cost as well. The larger units are handmade and tend to be expensive, and all types share the common defect of losing transparency with age, as a result of minute scratches that are almost inevitably incurred when removing abrasive diatomaceous growths from the front 'glass.' However, these tanks are nontoxic and not prone to corrosion.

The marine-quality stainless-steel-framed tanks are ranked next in this list of available aquaria. Because of the cost of such high-grade steel, these tanks are never cheap. They are strong, nontoxic, noncorrodible (providing the steel is truly marine quality) and, if properly made, will probably outlive ten tanks from the preceding categories. The reasons they are not at the head of the list are that they are enormously

Glass-fronted fiberglas tanks have been specially designed for use as marine aquaria.

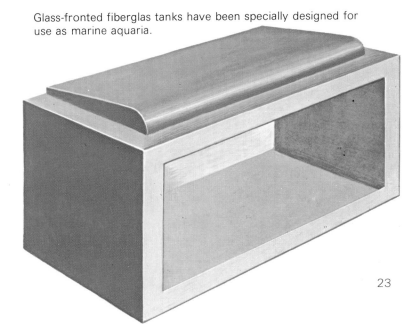

23

expensive, and heavy. Moreover, some people find their somewhat flashy appearance objectionable.

Finally, we come to the most recent development of all, the fiberglas-reinforced plastic tank, with a true glass front bonded to the plastic frame with silicone-rubber sealant. In this tank, all but one of all the desirable qualities are embodied as follows:
(1) low weight;
(2) nontoxic;
(3) noncorrodible;
(4) good appearance;
(5) high heat retention;
(6) can be made in almost any color or finish;
(7) high strength (i.e., heavy decorative objects can be used).

The discerning reader will have noticed that the omitted desirable quality is 'low cost.' These aquaria are handmade at the moment and are consequently expensive, but plans

A 'built-in' marine aquarium forms a fascinating decorative asset to a room. An all-glass tank is shown (*left*).

silicone adhesive seal

are already being considered to have them mass produced.

Such are the available containers. Not every reader will agree to the sequence of desirability used above, but it is hoped that a sufficiently unbiased appraisal of the relative attributes of each tank has been given.

Heaters and thermostats

Today, most brands of heaters and thermostats on the market are well made. Even the initial problems experienced by the manufacturers of the latest innovation—the combined heater and thermostat—have now been solved. Therefore the question is not which brand of equipment to purchase but rather the choice of the type of heating equipment that will serve one's requirements best.

In choosing a heater the major problem is one of matching the wattage of the instrument to the volume of water to be heated, taking into account the general temperature of the room in which the aquarium is to be located. This is a very important consideration, for an aquarium located in an unheated room will obviously require more heating in a given period of time than would the same aquarium in a modern, centrally heated room. A good general rule to apply is one 100-watt heater for an aquarium volume of 20 gallons in a normally heated room, or one 150-watt heater for the same volume in an unheated or poorly heated room. This is a lower wattage-to-volume ratio than many authors have suggested but I shall justify these figures shortly.

The choice of a thermostat is a little more difficult because of the great variety of these instruments now available. Generally speaking, if money is no object, I would advise the purchase of an external-fitting clip-on thermostat of superior manufacture with a wattage rating up to 2,000 watts. Such an instrument would be able to cope with the temperature regulation of up to 20 tanks, each with 100-watt heaters, assuming that the novice aquarist becomes thoroughly absorbed with his hobby. If the beginner is certain that he will not become quite so involved, then a cheaper external thermostat of similar design rated at 500 watts will provide adequate reserve. For those people who are certain that they will never have more than the one marine aquarium, a small, moderately priced, 200-watt internal-fitting instrument enclosed in a glass tube will be adequate.

The reason why a slightly lower than normal wattage-to-volume ratio has been suggested can now be explained. The only parts of the heater-thermostat combination liable to wear are the platinum-coated contact breakers in the thermostat. It follows, therefore, that the less these points have to open and close the better. A low-wattage heater will have to stay on longer to produce a unit quantity of heat, but it must not be assumed that more electricity is consumed. A high-wattage heater running for a short time uses just as much electricity as a low-wattage unit running for a longer time.

If you decide to use a separate heater and thermostat, you must ensure that the electrical connection between the two instruments is well insulated with nylon tape and/or sealed with silicone sealer. Salt water is a good conductor of electricity and finds its way into the least convenient places.

The ideal means of heating an aquarium employs a combined heater and thermostat. With these combined instru-

A combined heater and thermostat (*top*) and an external-fitting clip-on thermostat (*bottom*).

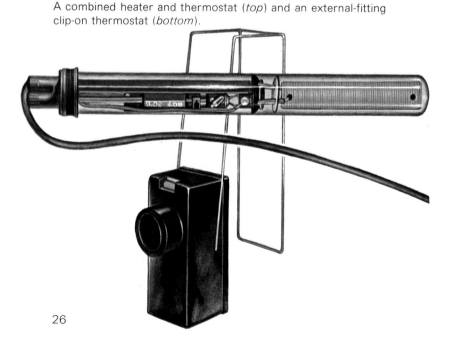

ments, there is only one lead carrying current; this lead, fitted with a plug, goes straight into the outlet (wall or extension), which should be above water level where possible.

Thermometers

An all-glass thermometer is ideal for the marine aquarium. The instrument should be fixed to the inside glass surface of one of the aquarium sides as unobtrusively as possible. Such instruments are generally attached to the glass by means of a synthetic rubber (or nontoxic plastic) disc. It is particularly important that the thermometer used in the marine aquarium has no metallic parts exposed to the salt water.

It is worth paying a little extra for a truly accurate thermometer, as many of the cheaper models frequently show an error of plus or minus 5° F (3° C). This is not important, of course, if the deviation from accuracy is linear (i.e., is constant throughout the range of temperature readings). In this case, you can compare the defective instrument's reading with that of a high-accuracy instrument and, noting the inaccuracy, compensate accordingly whenever you take a reading. The keen marine aquarist will soon get into the

Separate heater (*top*) and thermostat (*bottom*) and an all-glass thermometer with adhesive disc (*left*).

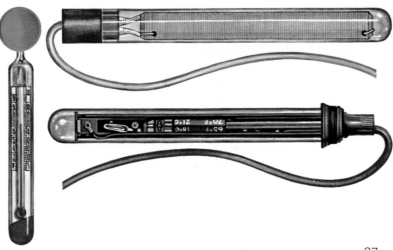

27

habit of checking the temperature of the water every time he feeds his animals. A marine aquarium for tropical life-forms requires a water temperature of $74° - 78°$ F ($24° - 26°$ C).

Air pumps

Two types of pumps are available to the marine aquarist:

(1) Vibrator pumps. These units are undoubtedly the cheapest and most maintenance-free of the air supply equipment under consideration. A vibrator pump requires no oiling, is fairly silent, delivers a very smooth (i.e., 'nonlumpy') supply of air and gives very good value in terms of cubic inches of air delivered per watt of electricity consumed. The most powerful units rate at about 30 watts and will thus consume one kilowatt hour of power only after they have been run nonstop for roughly 33 hours. It is important to keep the small absorbent cotton air filter clean, since an accumulation of dust under the rubber flap-valves, which control the admission and removal of air through the valve block, seriously reduces the air output of the pump.

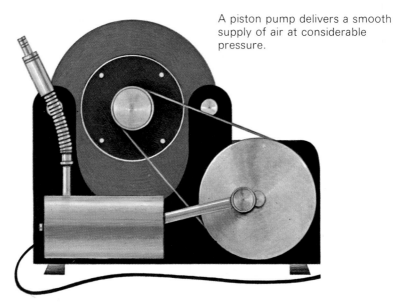

A piston pump delivers a smooth supply of air at considerable pressure.

Very efficient high-powered rotary pumps will soon be available to marine aquarists.

(2) **Piston pumps.** Although considerably more expensive, piston pumps have the advantage of delivering more air at greater pressure than average-priced vibrator pumps. The earlier piston pumps were of all-metal construction and needed frequent lubrication of moving parts; however, modern units usually make use of self-lubricating plastics. This has removed the need for frequent attention and brought about a reduction in noise level.

We may soon see the appearance of high-powered miniature rotary blowers which should provide greater volumes of air in unit time than air pumps currently available, although the pressure at which the air is delivered is unlikely to be as great.

Water filters
Broadly speaking, all currently available filtration equipment may be placed into one of the following categories:

(1) **Power filters.** As the name suggests, in these units the water passes through the filter media under power. The power is supplied by an electric motor (suitably isolated from contact with the salt water) which drives a plastic impeller fan.

The advantage of these units is that they move large volumes of water in a short space of time, which is exactly what is required for marine fishes. Furthermore, the power available means that the water can be forced through the minute inter-fiber spaces created by packing manmade fiber 'wool' into the filter chamber. In addition to the high degree of *mechanical filtration* (see pages 14 and 15) conferred by this means, some degree of *biochemical filtration* can be obtained through the placement of highly activated charcoal in the filter chamber. Activitated charcoal has the ability to adsorb certain organic gases and even low-molecular-weight organic solids in the water. It will also remove from solution the phenol-related yellowish-colored compounds so characteristic of old sea water, thus acting as a decolorizer.

(2) Filters utilizing airlifts. Although several types of filters using the airlift principle will be discussed, by far the most important of these to the marine aquarist is the undergravel filter.

The undergravel, or subsand, filter is of paramount importance in the marine aquarium. Once the gravel covering such a filter has 'ripened' (i.e., given rise to an enormous population of aerobic nitrifying bacteria), it is almost impossible to foul the water thereafter. These bacteria are able to oxidize the organic wastes produced as excreta by the marine animals, as well as the decomposition products from uneaten foods, into perfectly safe nitrate salts. These nitrates are then utilized by algae and diatoms in the synthesis of plant

to tank

water from tank

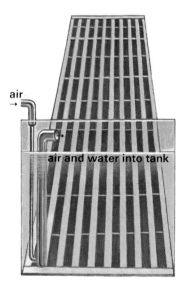

A power filter (*left*) and an undergravel filter utilizing an airlift (*right*) provide both mechanical and biochemical filtration.

air

air and water into tank

proteins. In the near future, de-ionizing resins will be developed that will be capable of the selective removal from solution of the organic toxins that cause discomfort and even death in marine animals, without profoundly affecting the pH of sea water. These resins will be used most effectively in a power filter but it is doubtful whether, for sheer low cost, long life, safety and the absence of maintenance, they will ever replace the undergravel filter as a means of detoxification of sea water.

In contrasting the rival merits of the power filter and the high-efficiency seawater undergravel filter, the most apparent difference is one of cost. A good power filter is costly and needs frequent servicing with expensive new filter materials. A good undergravel filter can be cheaply made in a home workshop or can be purchased at a relatively low cost. A power filter is operated by a complex electric motor whereas an undergravel filter is operated by an air pump, which is not likely to need repairs beyond annual replacement of the inexpensive rubber diaphragm. The undergravel filter does not remove the microscopic plankton life-forms from the water needed by such filter-feeding invertebrates as tubeworms, corals and sponges, whereas the power filter does do this. On the other hand, charcoal is easily used in a power filter and this is very helpful in sea water management.

To summarize, if the prospective marine aquarist can afford only one filter for his aquarium, he should buy or make a powerful undergravel filter. If on the other hand, money is not an important consideration and he wishes to study only marine fishes and nonfilter-feeding invertebrates such as anemones, crabs, shrimps, sea urchins, cowries and so on, then he should purchase *both* an undergravel filter and a power filter. For the vast majority of middle-income marine aquarists, a good compromise is a powerful undergravel filter and an external-fitting, airlift-operated filter of the type to be described next.

Bubble-up external filters. These are modestly priced and yet surprisingly efficient little external filters. They can be filled with charcoal and nylon 'wool' and are thus capable of giving both the decolorizing action and the higher degree of

31

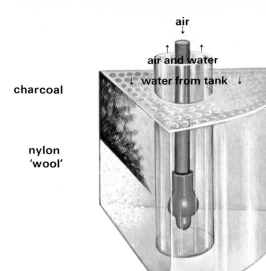

air

↑ ↑
air and water

↓ water from tank ↓

charcoal

nylon
'wool'

An internal bubble-up filter fits
into a bottom corner of the tank.

mechanical filtration lacking with an undergravel filter. They are operated by a small, cheap air pump and so have neither the high cost, complexity or need for frequent maintenance that is necessary with the motor-driven filter.

Bubble-up internal filters. Although they are quite effective and very cheap, these little units have both a low turnover rate and an unattractive appearance. They can be hidden behind rocks and shells, but these decorative items will have to be removed continually to determine the condition of the filter materials. If used at all, they are best confined to the quarantine tank where appearance is not as important.

Surface-fitting corner filters. Exactly the same criticisms apply to these filters as to the last described, except that these units are even more difficult to hide.

Filter media. Generally speaking, the only filter medium that is used with an undergravel filter is carefully graded gravel, preferably along with a layer of pH buffering material of suitable size, such as crushed coral, oyster shell or limestone gravel. With all the other types of filters discussed above, filter media can be highly activated carbon, nylon 'wool' and de-ionizing resins. In addition, a new filter medium has re-

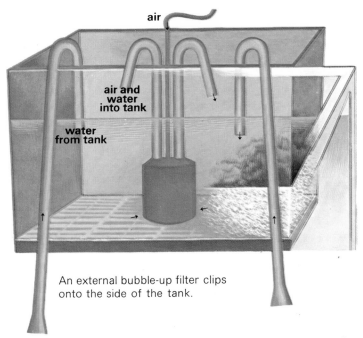

air

air and
water
into tank

water
from tank

An external bubble-up filter clips
onto the side of the tank.

cently appeared on the market for use in power filters only.
This has an interstitial lattice-work which is so fine that not
even bacteria nor motile algae can pass through it.

The ozonizer

The oxygen we breathe is made up of molecules containing
two atoms (i.e., the normal molecular state of oxygen).
However, if oxygen gas is passed through a very high-tension
electric field, the atoms regroup into threes, forming the
rare and unstable tri-atomic molecule called ozone. This
poisonous gas is one of the most powerful oxidizing agents
known to man and is a potent bactericide. It is of tremendous
value to the aquarist preferring a practically sterile tank (see
page 38) because it is his only means of oxidizing ammonia
to nitrites and nitrites to the harmless nitrates. To aquarists
preferring more natural marine systems, it is of value because
of its prophylactic and therapeutic value as a bactericide,
although the gas must be used with caution to avoid the lethal
effects on nitrifying, gravel-dwelling bacteria. There are
many other positive values of ozone in the marine aquarium;

however, the reader should not assume he cannot succeed as a marine aquarist without an ozonizer. Nothing could be farther from the truth.

The protein skimmer

It has long been common knowledge among specialists in sewage treatment that if minute air bubbles foam through water with a high organic waste content (such as raw sewage or sea water fouled by inexpert feeding or dead animals), many of the organic chemicals responsible for this pollution will migrate to the surface of the air bubbles. When the bubbles reach the surface, they congregate to form a stable foam. The greater the degree of organic pollution in the water, the more stable the foam. The beginner will do well to realize that one of the earliest symptoms of incipient fouling is the presence of just such a foam on the surface of the water. If some means could be devised of collecting this foam and allowing it to collapse into liquid which could then be thrown away, fouling of the aquarium water could be prevented. The diagram on the opposite page shows just such an apparatus, usually called a protein skimmer. To the aquarist possessing a high-turnover-rate undergravel filter it is of academic interest only, because the nitrifying bacteria living in the gravel of the filter will prevent all but the most persistent pollution.

The ultraviolet sterilizer

This is a device that is operated efficiently only by a power filter. Water from the power filter delivery tube circulates around a source of ultraviolet radiation. This radiation is lethal even in small doses to bacteria and protozoa responsible for diseases in aquarium fishes, but unfortunately it is equally lethal to the vast majority of other planktonic organisms, many of which are used as food by filter-feeders. As a prophylactic device (i.e., a means of preventing disease), such a unit may have its uses, but it will obviously be unable to prevent a disease if the reproductive rate of the pathogen is faster than the turnover rate of the power filter supplying the sterilizer with water, as is often the case.

A protein skimmer (*left*) and an ultraviolet sterilizer (*right*)

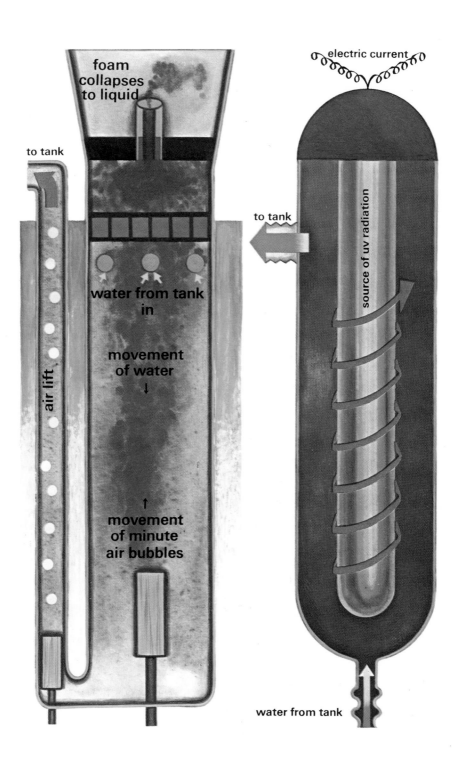

CREATING A MARINE AQUARIUM

The natural system

The natural system of maintaining a marine aquarium is an attempt to create as closely as possible a miniature environment identical in every important respect to the living coral reef. This system eschews all artificial aids to seawater management except one, and this exception means that the natural system is not, in fact, truly natural. We have already seen that few marine animals will tolerate stagnant sea water. Recognizing this fact as inescapable, the aquarist maintain-

An established natural system marine aquarium

ing his tank on the natural system always uses at least aeration as a means of creating some movement in the water.

The system was originally called the natural system because its adherents refuse the assistance of all manmade filtration aids, relying simply on the living coral-reef filter-feeders such as sponges, living corals, tubeworms and bryozoa to clean the water (i.e., to effect mechanical filtration). Biochemical filtration in such an aquarium is carried out only by the nitrifying bacteria coating every solid surface inside the unit making contact with the salt water. Since there is no undergravel filtration, a thick gravel bed cannot be used because there is the danger that uneaten food and excreta may decompose anaerobically in the gravel to produce poisonous gases such as hydrogen sulphide and methane. Without a thick gravel bed with an enormous surface area available for populations of nitrifying bacteria, the nitrifying potential of the tank is very low.

The foremost and original exponent of this system was Lee Chin Eng of Djakarta, Indonesia. Unfortunately, what many students of his method in the United States and Europe did not realize was that should anything go wrong in such a biosystem, such as accidental overfeeding or an unnoticed death, the nitrification potential is so minute that massive, unmanageable pollution would be the swift result. In a short time all the animals would be dead.

Setting up such a marine aquarium is very simple because the only items of equipment needed inside the tank are a heater and thermostat and an air-stone or wooden diffuser block. All manner of 'living stones' (i.e., pieces of coral rock heavily encrusted with invertebrate animals and various algae), are grouped in the aquarium to suit the aesthetic sensitivities of the aquarist. Various larger invertebrates of sessile or semisessile nature are then strategically placed in the tank. These can include anemones, live coral heads, tubeworms, clams and sponges. Next, various algae and higher marine plants such as eelgrass are included, and lastly, the moving invertebrates, such as starfishes, sea urchins, nudibranchs, cowries and conches, crayfishes, prawns, shrimps and crabs are added. After allowing a few days for the system to settle down, the fishes can be added.

The seminatural system

I am convinced that the seminatural system is the most economical and most successful method of seawater management. This system has been successfully elaborated since originally conceived in 1962 (see *The New Seaquarium System* by G. F. Cox), but basically the idea remains centered around a high-turnover-rate undergravel filter as the most efficient means yet devised of achieving rapid and total nitrification of toxic nitrogenous wastes. Many tropical freshwater aquarists who have attempted to utilize the author's filtration systems in their aquaria have reported very poor plant growth, no doubt caused by the rapid and unnatural circulation of water around the plant roots. However, this does not appear to have any adverse effects on the holdfasts, or base, of the marine algae cultured in marine aquaria. The advantages of the seminatural system are as follows:

(1) There is a massive nitrification potential, making fouling of the water almost impossible after the normal maturation period for the gravel (between 30 and 60 days).

(2) The aquarist is able to use a bed of gravel natural in appearance, without the danger of anaerobic decomposition of uneaten foods and excreta producing poisonous gases.

(3) Expensive and ugly pieces of apparatus, such as protein skimmers and power filters, are avoided, although the latter may be used if no filter-feeding invertebrates are to be cultured.

(4) If the airlift of the undergravel filter is brought above water level, a considerable degree of water aeration is achieved as a bonus.

(5) The water-movement system depends solely on the air supplied by a cheap, trouble-free vibrator-type air pump, although other types of air supply could be used with comparable success. The significance is that the only thing which can go wrong with a vibrator air pump is a punctured diaphragm, provided that the air-filter wool is kept clean. A replacement diaphragm for even the most expensive air pump on the market is very reasonably priced.

Provided due precautions are taken, the considerable advantages conferred by the intelligent use of ozone may be enjoyed using this system. The precautions really consist of ensuring that no ozone bubbles are carried down into the

A marine aquarium
maintained under the
seminatural system

gravel, because these would destroy the valuable nitrifying
bacteria coating every particle. To avoid this, the airlift should
not open above, but as near to the water level as possible.

The clinical system

There is no undergravel filtration in a marine aquarium
maintained under the clinical system and so, for the reasons
already outlined, there can be no gravel in the tank. Algal

and diatomaceous growths are prevented from gaining a foothold on the corals, shells and rocks in the aquarium by the periodic bleaching of these items in a commercially prepared bleach solution. The water in the tank is virtually plankton-free because of the 24-hour use of power filtration, which ensures that no filter-feeding invertebrates can survive. The aquarist is usually committed to a partial or total water change every few months, so the nitrate and phosphate levels of the salt water are never high enough to support growth of higher algae such as *Codium, Enteromorpha, Ulva* and so on. However, provided ozone is used at the very high level necessary to maintain the ammonia and nitrite content of the water within tolerable limits, extremely successful results will be obtained by the aquarist.

Probably the most successful exponent of this system in the world is the English aquarist, Roger Aked. This system was designed to Mr. Aked's specification by the brilliant Erwin Sander of Germany. Erwin Sander was probably the first person in the world to recognize the value of ozone in the marine aquarium, not just as an invaluable prophylactic agent, but also as an efficient oxidizer of nitrogenous toxins. Roger Aked's private collection of some 300 marine animals displayed in over 2,000 gallons of clear, synthetic sea water would put quite a few public aquaria to shame. The only water-management devices used are giant protein skimmers using heavily ozonized air as the foaming gas. After this treatment, the water passes through towers packed with highly activated charcoal before re-entering the tanks. With this apparatus, Mr. Aked has successfully cultured many difficult animals for three and four years (i.e., their probable natural life span on the reef). His system, however, was fantastically expensive to install and costs a small fortune to maintain. Using the seminatural system detailed earlier, many new marine aquarists have established tanks for a very reasonable outlay and have kept for comparable periods of time equally difficult, if smaller, animals.

The tank is usually typified by the use of ion-exchange resin-packed power filters, ozonizers, ultraviolet sterilizers, protein skimmers and 'whiter-than-white' corals. Occasionally the extremist will go to the unforgivable lengths of equipping his aquarium with busty mermaids, dyspeptic green plastic frogs, sunken galleons and questing divers and even plastic violet dahlias. Thankfully, many of these aberrations appear to be waning in popularity.

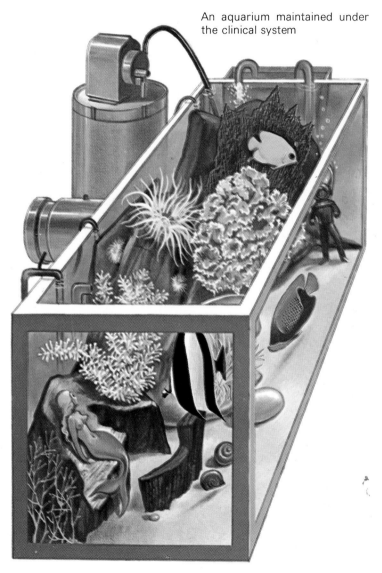

An aquarium maintained under the clinical system

FURNISHING THE MARINE AQUARIUM

The materials available to the marine aquarist for furnishing his aquarium are much more varied than those available to the freshwater aquarist, who is generally limited to plants, rockwork and attractively shaped pieces of dead wood. The marine aquarist has instead corals of enormous variety of form, sea shells of almost infinite variety of form and color, and such things as sea fans, gorgonian skeletons, sea urchin tests and, of course, the sessile and semisessile invertebrate animals themselves such as anemones and tubeworms.

The question of how to arrange a given selection of decorative objects is entirely one of personal choice. Two people will rarely agree on what constitutes beauty. I can only give guidelines as to what pleases me and trust that these views may find favor with the majority of marine aquarists.

Generally speaking, the first thing to do is to choose a striking centerpiece. This may be a giant pink conch shell, a particularly large and splendid coral head or even a large, well-figured minerally tested rock. Great care should be taken to ensure that this item is not placed in the geometrical center of the tank. A more well-balanced arrangement will result if such an object is placed one-third to two-fifths of the length of the tank from the end. All the other less significant objects can then be grouped around it to lead up to a 'crescendo'. Always try to group all pieces of the same species of coral together rather than scattering them all over the tank. Keep large shells well to the rear of the tank. Try to avoid pur-

Arrangement of decorative items in a well-furnished tank

chasing pieces of coral of the same height. Instead, buy at least one tall coral, such as branch or elkhorn coral, and use this off-center, toward the rear of the tank, to create an illusion of vertical depth in the aquarium.

There are many types of rocks suitable for use in a marine aquarium. I would urge one precaution in the selection and placement of rocks, however. Before risking the poisoning of a prized collection of animals, any unknown rockwork should first be scrubbed and then soaked in salt water for a month, after which pH and nitrite tests can be conducted on the water. When positioning rocks and corals, try to keep tall pieces to the rear third of the tank.

When placing decorative materials within the tank, bear in mind that almost all the true reef-dwelling species of fishes greatly appreciate the provision of suitably sized hiding places. Among the invertebrates, the octopus, mantis, Boxing Shrimps and crinoids (sea lilies or feather-stars) also welcome similar thoughtfulness.

Shells

Almost all mollusks, particularly the marine mollusks, have the ability to extract certain salts, mostly calcium and magnesium, from sea water. After altering these salts slightly, they secrete them as layer upon layer of hard calcareous solids. The resulting completed structure is called the shell and serves to protect the soft and therefore vulnerable tissues within. Eventually the animal which made the shell dies,

Arrangement of decorative items in a badly furnished tank

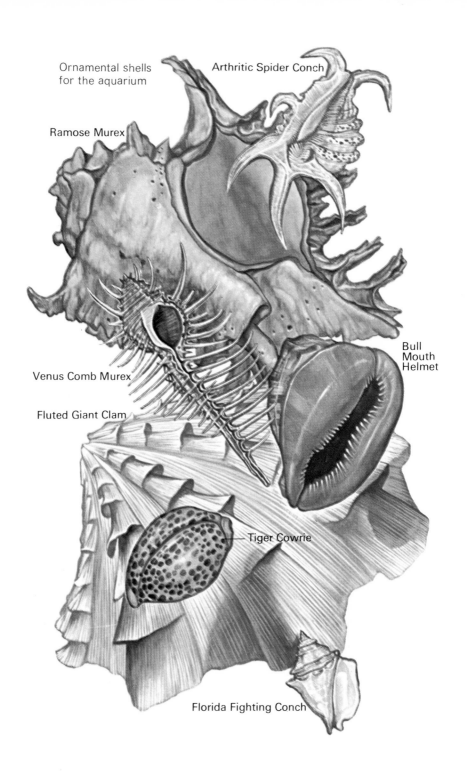

Ornamental shells
for the aquarium

Arthritic Spider Conch

Ramose Murex

Venus Comb Murex

Fluted Giant Clam

Bull
Mouth
Helmet

Tiger Cowrie

Florida Fighting Conch

either from natural causes or because of predation by various animals such as other mollusks, crustaceans, fishes such as the triggerfishes, reptiles, birds or mammals (including man). After dying, the resistant, inorganic shell is slowly worn away as it rolls over the sea bed.

The vast majority of shells used to decorate the marine aquarium are those of the univalve mollusks. Examples of the more common of these are the conus, cowrie, murex, cameo shells, batswings, spiders, scorpions and conches.

Certain shells of bivalve mollusks (i.e., mollusks which secrete a shell in two more or less distinct halves) are also used in the marine aquarium. The giant clams and the scallops are examples, but these are not nearly as intricate and attractive as shells of the univalve.

The sea shell in the marine aquarium has three functions:

(1) **Decoration.** The vast majority of tropical sea shells are large, colorful and beautiful in form and are therefore of aesthetic value as decorative items in the aquarium. Many of the newcomers to the hobby of marine aquarium keeping became interested via another very absorbing hobby — *conchology,* the study and collection of sea shells.

(2) **Refuge.** By imaginative placing within the aquarium, sea shells can be used to provide an intricate network of galleries and passages for use by nervous and shy fishes as 'hideouts' and nighttime resting places.

(3) *p*H **buffering.** The calcium and magnesium salts making up the shells are almost entirely the carbonate salts. As such they are invaluable aids for maintaining the water *p*H at the correct alkalinity.

A sea shell as sold by a dealer is rarely ready to be placed straight into the marine aquarium. All too often some part of the dead animal is trapped inside the shell, and this would quickly foul the water if placed in the tank. To avoid this possibility, all shells should be treated by being steeped in a bleach solution for three days, washed under a running tap for one hour and finally boiled in a stainless steel or enameled saucepan for two hours, prior to being put into the tank.

45

Corals

Many marine aquarists experienced in culturing delicate invertebrate organisms maintain several heads of live coral in their marine aquaria. The less-experienced aquarist uses dead corals for aquarium decor, provision of refuges and for the pH buffering effect these items produce as a bonus.

The vast coral reefs of the world have been built up painfully and slowly over hundreds of years by tiny colonial animals whose close relatives are the much larger anemones. The dead coral underlying today's living reef was formed hundreds of thousands of years ago; if one were to drill deep enough, coral stone would be reached which was formed hundreds of millions of years ago by the remote ancestors of the present-day coral polyps.

Coral polyps also have the ability to extract certain salts, mostly calcium carbonate, from sea water. They secrete these salts from surface cells, building up a stone-hard tube around themselves that protects them from predators and, if they are growing near the high-water mark on a shallow, sloping reef, from desiccation during the short period they are exposed to the tropical sun. These polyps are mostly colonial, and neighboring tubes fuse together to produce the relatively large structures we recognize as coral heads of various species.

When selecting pieces of coral to enhance the marine aquarium, it is better to 'shop' for pieces of the right size and shape to fill a preselected space, rather than buying coral on impulse and then attempting to force it into arbitrary places in the tank.

Generally speaking, the following hints may help regarding the positioning of the coral. Pieces of coral of the same species should be grouped together, and tall pieces kept to the rear of the tank. Try to build up to a high spot toward the rear of the tank which is well off-center, and introduce color in the tank decor by using organ pipe coral *(Tubifora)*. This is the only coral in which the calcareous skeleton itself is brightly colored. It is a vivid scarlet and is always a pleasant feature in any marine aquarium decor.

No matter how clean a piece of coral appears to be when purchased, it should always be cured in the manner given for treating shells. It is important that no smell of chlorine should persist on the coral when it is placed in the aquarium.

Rock and corals suitable for aquarium decor: 1. Finger Coral, 2. Lettuce Brain Coral, 3. Branch or Elkhorn Coral, 4. Rose Coral, 5. *Fungia* Coral and 6. Brain Coral

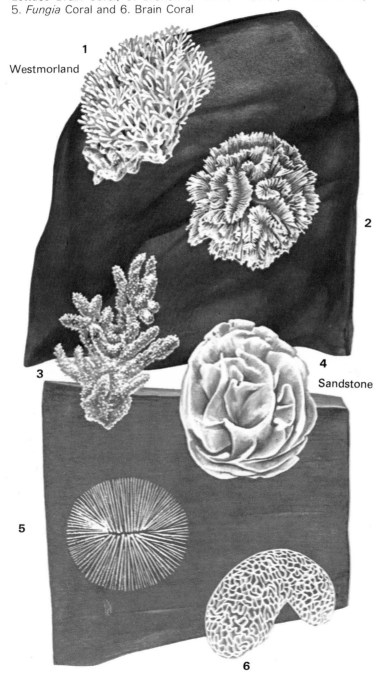

1

Westmorland

2

3

4

Sandstone

5

6

FISHES FOR THE AQUARIUM

Sharks and rays

Sharks and rays belong to a class of fishes known as the elasmobranchs. These fishes are all characterized by the possession of a cartilaginous, or gristly, rather than a bony skeleton. The lack of rigid internal structure means that the internal organs are not as securely anchored as in the bony fishes, and so great care must be taken when handling them out of water. Many small sharks and rays that refuse to feed in captivity do so because the viscera have been seriously dislocated by clumsy handling before the animals were sold to the collector.

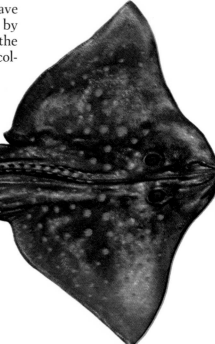

Thornback Ray

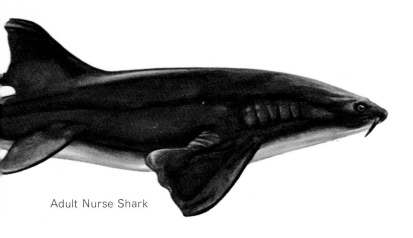

Adult Nurse Shark

Thornback Ray *(Raja clavata)*
This species can be readily kept in a large tank, since feeding presents few problems. This ray shows a marked preference for crustacean and molluscan flesh. It is unlikely that these fishes will ever accept dried foods, for they show interest only in fresh protein.

Nurse Shark *(Ginglymostoma cirratum)*
One of the few sharks suitable for culture in the marine home tank, the Nurse Shark is available in sizes down to 13 to 15 inches. It is impossible to obtain this species any smaller than this because the female is *ovoviviparous*. This means that although there is no placental development of the embryo as in mammals, the female is fertilized internally and the embryo develops within her body; at birth, the infant emerges as a fully formed dwarf version of the parents. This species can grow to around 14 feet in length, but seldom exceeds 20 inches when kept in a 6-foot, 120-gallon aquarium. Although the Nurse Shark is reputed not to be a man-eater, there are several well-authenticated accounts of serious attacks on young bathers in the Caribbean, usually caused by teasing of the adult sharks.

The Nurse Shark, being *demersal,* or bottom-dwelling, in habit, is one of the few members of the shark family that can breathe when stationary. The *pelagic* sharks, which move freely at all depths in the ocean, are, with a few exceptions, unable to breathe unless continually on the move.

Feeding Nurse Sharks in the marine aquarium presents few problems because they are scavengers and therefore have small appetites once acclimatized to the tank. Difficulties in starting them to feed can usually be overcome by offering squid, mussel or prawn flesh in the evening, when they become more active. They appear to rely almost entirely on their sense of smell to enable them to detect food. The sympathetic shark owner will bear this in mind in the early attempts at feeding, taking into account any currents in his tank when deciding where to drop the foodstuffs, so that the scent of the food is carried to the shark.

Bony fishes
Squirrelfishes or Soldierfishes (Family Holocentridae)
These fishes (genera *Holocentrus, Myripristis, et al.*) are primarily nocturnal in habit. This is indicated by their large eyes and, perhaps less obviously, by their bright red coloration; most nocturnal reef fishes are predominantly red in color. A squirrelfish is a voracious predator and must never be trusted in a community with small fishes. However, once a specimen is well adjusted to aquarium life, it will learn to accept chunks of flesh, provided that it can see the food falling through the water. Few members of this genus will take static food particles from the floor of the aquarium, no matter how hungry they are.

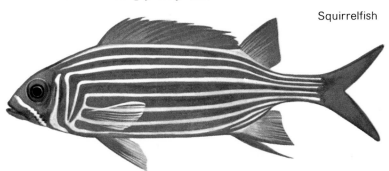

Squirrelfish

Seahorses and pipefishes (Family Syngnathidae)
Seahorses are often the first marine animals that the novice marine aquarist chooses for his tank. These fishes are undoubtedly of equestrian appearance, caused by the horselike

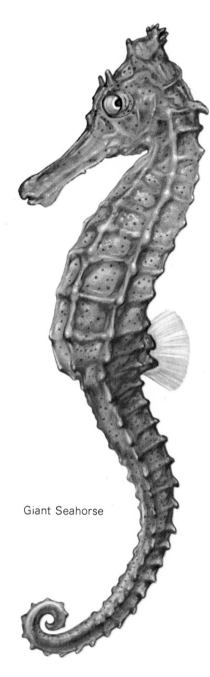

Giant Seahorse

form of the head and their deportment. The latter characteristic is produced because the normal posture of the body is in the vertical plane with the head held at right angles.

Throughout recorded history these unlikely looking animals have excited the curiosity of all who have seen them. Seahorses have featured in the design of coins, the signet ring of a Roman Emperor and the coats-of-arms of individuals and civic bodies. They also feature in the collections of fishes of almost every marine aquarist, at least until their several disadvantages become apparent. Prime among these is their refusal to eat anything except small living crustaceans such as brine shrimps (*Artemia*), although a few individuals will learn to accept *Daphnia*. Nevertheless, aquarists are advised against the purchase of these slow-moving, slow-witted animals because of this feeding problem. The great majority of seahorses imported from the Philippines and Singapore are an undistinguished muddy-brown color, although red, yellow and white specimens do sometimes occur.

51

Banded Pipefish

Related pipefishes from the South Pacific are certainly more active and entertaining to observe in a natural-system marine aquarium than seahorses but, again, they are essentially macroplankton feeders with the same demanding food requirements.

Some specimens of the Banded Pipefish will show a greater degree of adaptability under aquarium conditions than others. For example, if three pipefishes from the same area were purchased from the same dealer, it is likely that one or even two will learn to eat small live *Daphnia* added to the tank, whereas the third specimen will starve to death unless offered living marine crustaceans, such as brine shrimp larvae or tiny sand-hoppers.

However, even the most adaptable pipefish, seahorse or shrimpfish will steadfastly refuse all food unless it is alive, moving, and of the correct size to trigger off the feeding response. Needless to say, the unique nutritional requirements of seahorses, pipefishes and shrimpfishes always mean that feeding is something of a headache.

In order to conserve these food supplies, particularly

during the winter months when such food is not so readily available, it is advisable not to include any other animals within the aquarium which would compete for the food. Most small coral-reef fishes, particularly juvenile butterfly fishes and angelfishes, relish small crustaceans and newly born live-bearer fry.

Shrimpfishes (Family Centriscidae)

Shrimpfishes are related to the seahorses and are also characterized by a strong exoskeleton of horny material. A much more striking feature is their curious habit of swimming permanently upside down. Furthermore, the extraordinary mobility and incessant activity of their expressive eyes, coupled with their head-down swimming position, makes the fishes look as if they are forever searching for some treasured possession recently lost.

Again, it must be said that unless a well-matured natural-system tank and thousands of brine shrimp larvae are available daily, these enchanting creatures should never be removed from their reef homes.

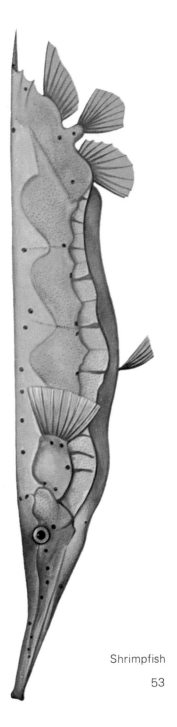

Shrimpfish

53

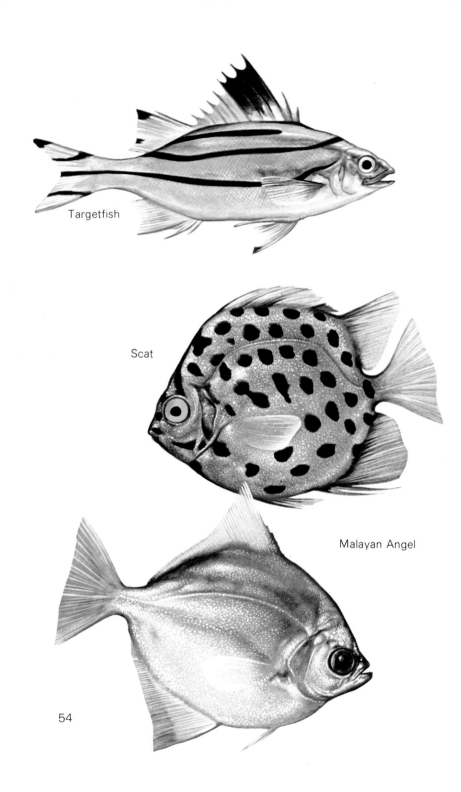

Targetfish

Scat

Malayan Angel

54

Brackish water fishes

Targetfish *(Therapon jarbus)*

These fishes, also known as Tigerfishes or Crescent Perches, are equally at home in pure salt water or brackish water, and although they may be maintained successfully in fresh water they seldom appear to be fully at ease. They are probably the hardiest of all fishes that can be kept in a marine aquarium, feeding with great exuberance on all foods. They can become boisterous and may subdue the more delicate true reef fishes, such as the butterfly fishes, causing the latter to hide and slowly starve to death. They are almost disease-free, very long-lived and grow rapidly. They are usually low-priced and so are in excellent first choice for the novice aquarist. They are not brilliantly colored but because they frquently school, a dozen or so in a large tank is an impressive sight.

Scat *(Scatophagus argus)*

This fish's systematic name unfortunately translates into English as the 'Hundred-eyed Muck-eater'. This name was acquired because the first specimens examined by Western ichthyologists were found to have stomachs full of excrement. Such unsavory feeding habits, however, are certainly not characteristic of this species when it is provided with more attractive fare. In the marine aquarium Scats do not prove as hardy as Targetfishes or Malayan Angels. Still, they have been kept for more than four years by relative beginners in the field.

Malayan Angel *(Monodactylus argenteus)*

In the marine aquarium, Malayan Angels (or Diamond Fishes or Moonfishes) should be kept in groups of three or more. On the reef they occur in dense shoals of up to a thousand fishes, moving with uncanny precision. They tend to be bullied in the aquarium unless provided with adequate retreats. Their low price, readiness to accept even the most mundane foodstuffs and strong resistance to diseases makes them another ideal choice for the beginner. Their close relatives from the West African coast, *Monodactylus sebae,* are more attractive but not as hardy in captivity.

Six-striped Grouper

Since these three species of fishes are occasionally sold by dealers from brackish and even freshwater tanks, the specific gravity of the water in which they are bought should be carefully checked. If the specific gravity differs greatly from that in the marine aquarist's tank, this imbalance should be slowly corrected by gradually adding tank water to the plastic bag in which the fishes were carried home.

Groupers (Family Serranidae)

The following six fishes are strongly recommended to the more ambitious beginner. They are all very hardy, colorful, will eat almost any form of fresh protein and are not particularly susceptible to diseases.

In the wild state, the grouper, or rock cod, lives a very leisurely life, punctuated at intervals by sudden powerful lunges from its rocky lairs with mouth agape to engulf an imprudent passerby. In the marine aquarium, however, this characteristic behavior may be significantly modified. The relatively high intelligence, good memory and excellent eyesight shared by members of the grouper family means that they soon come to recognize their owner and commence the unusual behavior of swimming up and down in the open as soon as he enters the room.

Six-striped Grouper *(Grammistes sexlineatus)*

The Six-striped Grouper is a very intelligent fish. At its juvenile size, about 1½ to 2½ inches, it is safe with almost any other fishes. However, in common with others of its family, it has an exceedingly large mouth, a characteristic which,

56

Jewel-spotted Grouper

as the fish grows larger, may be the beginning of the end for the smaller damselfishes, clownfishes and others which share the tank.

Jewel-spotted Grouper *(Cephalopholis argus)*

The wide range of this species has given rise to some variation in coloring, but broadly speaking, a reddish-brown background color scattered with bright blue circles is typical of the species. Like all the groupers, it swims slowly by alternate movements of the pectoral fins, using only the powerful back muscles to thresh the tail fin when the forward-lunge mechanism is triggered. In this respect, the feeding habits of the groupers are very similar to those of the fresh-water pike. In captivity, the grouper usually (but not always) realizes that continued taking of small live fishes for food is unnecessary, and after a few days it is ready to receive small chunks of any kind of flesh.

Cephalopholis boenacki

As with other groupers, this species soon learns to accept some form of fresh meat, such as prawn, shrimp, squid, well-washed steak, liver and so on. This species is particularly hostile to other fishes of its own genus and species. Even a male and female will be mutually hostile if placed together out of the breeding season. Thus it is preferable to keep them individually rather than in pairs. Many marine fishes, and the groupers are no exception, have the ability to quickly change their coloration to match a particular shade in the environment or to display an emotion. An

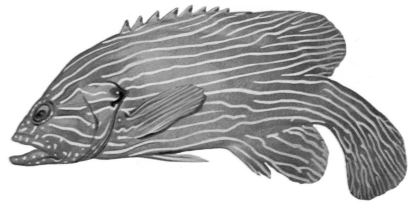

Cephalopholis boenacki

indication of the hardiness of this fish is its tremendously successful ability to colonize the tropical oceans of the world. *Cephalopholis boenacki* has been reported from places as far apart as East Africa and Singapore.

As with other large groupers, feeding presents no problem. When the fish has settled into its new home, it should be given a day or so before food is offered. The new owner should be sympathetic enough to realize that capture, air freight and introduction to aquarium life are disturbing experiences for most fishes. For a highly territorial animal like the grouper, which derives psychological security from total familiarity with a small area, this sudden removal into an entirely different habitat may border on the traumatic.

Epinepholus flavocaeruleus
This is perhaps the most attractive of all the groupers. The body coloration of this fish both in range and tone of blue is almost identical to the totally unrelated Powder-blue Surgeonfish (*Acanthurus leucosternon,* see pages 92 and 94). It is interesting to speculate why two fishes of very different habitat should have such similar coloration. The grouper is a territorial, lurking animal that is fond of caves and is highly predatory, while the surgeonfish is an open water, shoaling fish, feeding on algae and macroplankton. Whatever the reason, aquarists must surely rejoice at the generosity of nature

58

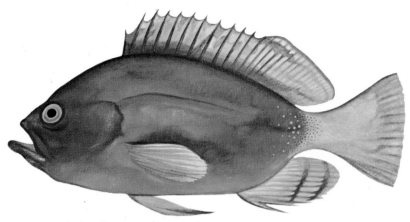

Epinepholus flavocaeruleus

in producing two fishes of such exquisite coloration.

As with other groupers, fishes new to the aquarium should be allowed two or three days to familiarize themselves with their new environment before feeding is attempted. After this time, their fear of their owner and the new territory will have been overcome by the pangs of hunger. On offering sizable chunks of fresh protein, the owner will be rewarded by the usual grouper-lunge as the fish spots the descending piece of meat and, with unbelievable speed, rushes from its lair. The groupers may be kept in community with other coral-reef fishes, provided that all the other fishes are at least as large as the grouper and preferably larger.

Pantherfish *(Chromileptis altivelis)*

The Pantherfish is not brilliantly colored but is nonetheless characterized by a most striking pattern of blue-black circular spots on a rich grayish-brown background. A marked feature of this fish is the ludicrously small proportion of the head in relation to the remainder of the body. The chromatic tints of turquoise, gold and silver refracted by the fins are of indescribable beauty when the fish is caught at the correct angle, and the eyes radiate emerald-green malevolence like those of a pagan idol. However, this baleful expression is counterbalanced by the most comical paddling of the absurdly large pectoral fins, and so the total impression on the observer is an amusing rather than fearful one. The Pantherfish will never-

Pantherfish

theless quickly eat any animal small enough to fit its enormous mouth.

When fishes of this species come to know their owner, they spend less of their time indulging in the classical grouper activity of lurking and may become quite bold, swimming almost continuously in the open spaces between corals and rocks. With its outlandishly large fins fully spread, a good-sized Pantherfish is an impressive sight when swimming prominently in the aquarium.

Cerise Grouper *(Variola louti)*
The grouper is a rare and treasured beauty in aquarists' tanks; it is not rare in the wild, but collectors experience extreme difficulty in extracting it from its lair and at the same time retaining all their fingers intact.

60

This fish's control of body color is highly developed, perhaps more than any other grouper. When at rest, it is an uninspiring russet-brown with the slightest hint of blue spots liberally scattered over its body. If a small live fish is introduced into the tank, a miraculous change in appearance occurs. Almost imperceptibly at first and then with gathering momentum, the fish's whole body becomes suffused with an indescribable shade of red. Small islets of sapphire-blue radiate a strange glow as the fish's body pulsates with light a few seconds before the 'grouper-lunge'. After capturing the fish, the grouper's colors subside until the next mealtime.

Cerise Grouper

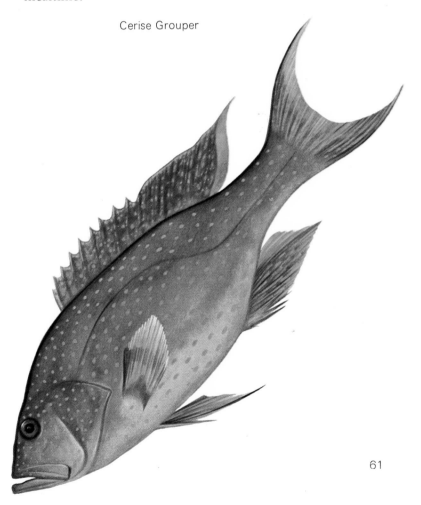

Wreckfish (*top*) and
Royal Gramma (*bottom*)

Wreckfishes (Family Anthiidae)
Wreckfish *(Anthias squamipinnis)*
This fish is available in two distinct forms which occupy the same territory on the same reef; this may well be sexual variation within the same species. To date, my collector has been unable to confirm this theory, since he has not witnessed any spawning activity in the species.

This fish has a manner of swimming reminiscent of *Amphiprion* species, to which it is not even distantly related. The whole body undulates with a slow sinewy grace as the large pectoral fins alternately paddle back and forth with seemingly little effect. A beginner not acquainted with this species could easily think that the fish was distressed because of its unusual mode of progress through the water.

Feeding a newly imported Wreckfish can be nerve-racking, as it can frequently be reluctant to begin taking dead foods in captivity. The first Wreckfish I ever caught came from a small reef off Mozambique. Although it survived the arduous 2,000-mile journey from the East African coast to Central Africa, once home it refused all food, even baby guppies, for nearly two weeks. One morning it accepted a guppy and, from then on, its progress to full acclimatization proceeded without interruption. After ten days on live guppies, followed by three days on freshly killed baby guppies, it accepted its first feeding of dead protein. This was a small piece of fresh steak impaled on the end of a toothpick. Because of this initial difficulty in feeding, I would not enthusiastically recommend this species to the beginning home aquarist.

Grammas (Family Grammidae)
Royal Gramma *(Gramma loreto)*
This beautifully colored fish was once believed to exist only in relatively deep water, below about 30 to 40 feet, in the Caribbean area. However, thanks to the efforts of collectors in the area, it has been found that the Royal Gramma exists in shallow water, 3 to 6 feet, but it is very difficult to detect because it swims upside down in caves and under ledges. It is as if the fish feels that its abdominal region is particularly vulnerable, and it seldom swims with the ventral surface

63

of its body more than a few inches away from a solid surface. It is carnivorous, and in the wild it probably feeds on various macroplankton (i.e., small crustaceans, larval and juvenile fishes, and so on). Comments regarding feeding are the same as for the previous species.

Cardinal Fishes (Family Apogonidae)
Cardinal fishes (*Apogon* spp) are quite hardy fishes that can be recommended to the beginner as excellent species with which to start, apart from the fact that they rarely accept dried food in captivity. Most species have to be fed small live fishes or, after a period in captivity, fresh protein such as minute pieces of earthworm, prawn and steak.

These species are mouth-breeders; that is to say, the fertilized eggs are retained in the parent's mouth for incubation. Because of this, cardinal fishes may be among the first species of marine fishes the aquarist may successfully breed in captivity.

The movement of cardinal fishes is strange in that it takes the form of short periods of slow forward motion followed by long ones of total inactivity. During this time, the dainty little creatures appear to be suspended in midwater in a slightly head-down attitude, as if hung by invisible threads.

Goatfishes (Family Mullidae)
The goatfishes of the genus *Pseudupeneus* rank with the Striped Catfish *(Plotosus anguillaris)* and the Thornback Ray *(Raja clavata)* as the few bottom scavengers suitable for the average-sized marine tank. However, the goatfishes are not noted for their beauty of form, though both the red and yellow species are very strikingly colored.

As befits most scavenging organisms, they have a very wide taste in foodstuffs. Food that no other self-respecting coral-reef fish would swim anywhere near is frequently snapped up from the bottom with a relish not easily disguised. However, this readiness of the fishes to dispose of surplus food must not be an excuse for laxness in tank management. Decaying organic matter lying around on the aquarium floor will not benefit either the goatfishes or any other occupants of the tank in the long run.

Batfishes (Family Platacidae)

The batfishes commonly available to the marine aquarist at this time are illustrated on the opposite page. They can present something of an enigma because of their curious inclination for flying into a panic at the slightest provocation when in unfamiliar surroundings. Once acclimatized, however, they have few equals; they have undemanding appetites, extremely high resistance to all diseases, a high rate of growth and aquarium longevity. These statements apply wholly to *Platax orbicularis*, slightly less so to *P. teira*, and slightly less still to the beautiful *P. pinnatus*. *Platax orbicularis* may even be regarded as a beginner's fish for those lucky enough to begin their hobby with large tanks, but *P. teira* should not be purchased until one has at least six months experience, whereas *P. pinnatus* should not be purchased by anyone who cannot afford to isolate two, three or more of these beautiful creatures on their own in at least an 80-gallon aquarium.

The batfish *P. orbicularis* will take any kind of fresh protein. At various times I have owned adaptable individuals who, when really hungry, would even take dried food. Specimens of *P. teira* will, however, only accept fresh meat such as prawn, heart, liver and so on, while *P. pinnatus* takes only live earthworms.

The batfishes soon learn to detect the vibrations and later the visual stimuli of the owner's approach to the aquarium. Even before the cover is raised, the hungry fishes may cavort at the water's surface in eager anticipation of the food to come.

For fishes that grow so large—specimens measuring 12 inches in fin span are not uncommon—batfishes appear defenseless and are at the mercy of the aquarium's 'bullies'. Most fishes lacking either sharp teeth and/or sharp spines show high-speed retreat as a defense system. The batfishes, however, seem to have been curiously neglected in the evolution of these defensive measures. The young fishes will often drift motionless in a current, closely resembling dead leaves or pieces of seaweed, but the adults have none of this guile and must presumably rely on some objectionable substance in their skin or mucus secretion to deter predators.

Angelfishes (Family Pomacanthidae)
Koran Angelfish *(Pomacanthus semicirculatus)*

This species of angelfish is probably more popular than any other from the Indo-Pacific. It is a very successful species, ranging from East Africa across the Indo-Pacific to Ceylon and into the Pacific Ocean to the Philippines. Unlike many other marine fishes with a wide range, there is surprisingly little variability in color and form within the species. It is almost impossible to differentiate between a specimen from Kenya and one from the Philippines. However, although little variation is seen among adult fishes, the variation in color pattern among developing juveniles within this genus is amazing; the illustration below shows some phases in the development. This phenomenon has created a great deal of confusion among amateur taxonomists. Animals of the same species but at different stages of development have been named as new species, and even attributed to different families.

The Koran Angelfish is an excellent aquarium fish, acclimatizing to the aquarium in only two or three days, and

Color variation in juvenile and adult forms of the Koran Angelfish

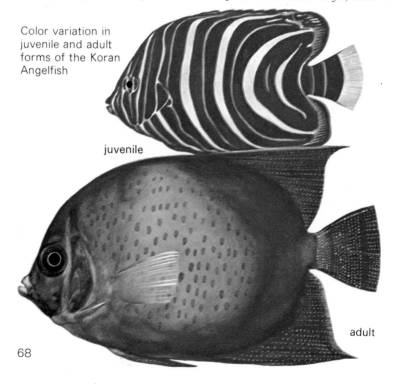

juvenile

adult

accepting all foods with eagerness. It is somewhat prone to *Saprolegnia* fungus disease (see page 152), but this clears up in a few hours if ozone medication is used.

Emperor Angelfish *(Pomacanthus imperator)*

The adult of this species is one of the most spectacular marine fishes. When familiar with its surroundings, the Emperor, or Imperial, Angelfish moves effortlessly around the marine aquarium with a sense of majesty and circumstance which prompted early German marine aquarists to bestow the name 'Kaiserfische' on the species.

The Emperor Angelfish is a little more demanding than the previous species with regard to water quality, and even the slightest trace of nitrite in the water seems to debilitate the animal, making it prone to diseases which it would otherwise resist. *Benedenia* (see page 152) is a commonly seen infection among newly imported specimens, or those kept in less than ideally pure water. This condition is easily cured if the animal is promptly transferred to ex-

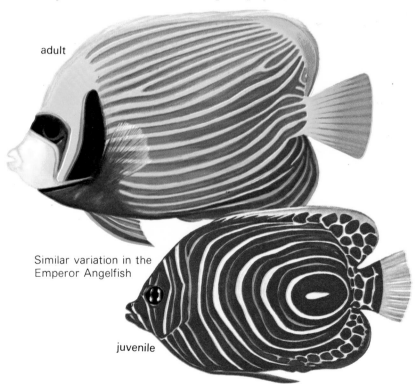

adult

Similar variation in the
Emperor Angelfish

juvenile

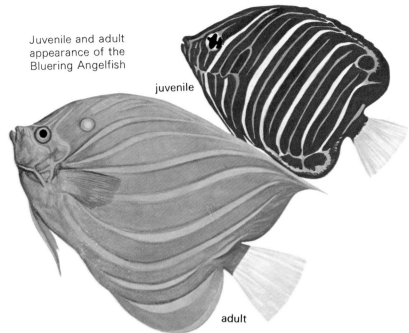

Juvenile and adult appearance of the Bluering Angelfish

juvenile

adult

ceptionally clean water and treated with Cuprazin or sodium sulphamezathine. The correct dosage is one teaspoonful of solution to 10 gallons of water. If the latter treatment is used, the fish should be transferred to fresh sea water five days after the disappearance of symptoms, to avoid the possibility of massive kidney damage. Live foods may be neccessary to tempt the Emperor Angelfish to begin feeding in captivity, but it will soon move on to various forms of fresh protein.

Bluering Angelfish *(Pomacanthus annularis)*
The similarity between juvenile forms of this fish and the preceding two species can be a source of great confusion to the beginner, as the illustrations show. All three fishes have a juvenile patterning of white lines on a radiant blue background. The following points may help the beginner to be certain of which species he is buying in the absence of expert advice from a dealer. In the Koran Angelfish the white stripes are slightly curved or shaped, but they are much more curved with one near the tail forming a completely closed ellipse in the Emperor Angelfish. In the Bluering Angelfish the white stripes are almost straight, with only the ends

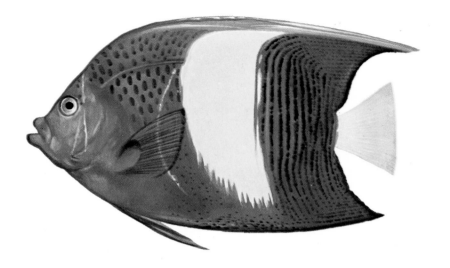

Juvenile and adult forms of the Purple Moon Angelfish are similar to each other in appearance.

curving inward slightly toward the tail.

Foods offered initially to the Bluering Angelfish should be live foods such as freshly sterilized mussel cut into shreds, chopped earthworm, whiteworm and live brine shrimps. The healthy Bluering Angelfish will, however, quickly graduate to more convenient forms of fresh protein.

Purple Moon Angelfish *(Pomacanthus maculosus)*
Although not so spectacularly colored as the previous species, the adult specimen of *P. masculosus* has beautiful elongated tips to the posterior edges of the dorsal and anal fins and is a most graceful swimmer. It is perhaps the most hardy of all the larger angelfishes, having a high resistance to disease and a very adaptable appetite. Although it is not one of the cheapest of the angelfishes, it can be strongly recommended to the beginner after he has gained initial experience with damselfishes and clownfishes.

Feeding presents no difficulties whatsoever and although fishes are initially very shy, after seven to ten days in the aquarium they will continually display their pleasing colors at the front of the tank. All foods are eagerly accepted. The

71

very similar angelfish *P. asfur,* from the same small area of the North Kenya coast up to the Red Sea, is easily distinguished from the Purple Moon Angelfish by its bright yellow tail.

Black, or Gray, Angelfish *(Pomacanthus arcuatus)*

This species and the very similar French Angelfish are native to the Caribbean area. In common with other marine aquarium fishes from this area, they appear to be more than usually prone to *Lymphocystis* disease. This may be because the virus causing the disease is totally or nearly absent from the Caribbean, so that the fishes from that area have not developed resistance to it. Imported Caribbean species rarely develop the creamy white cysts caused by the *Lymphocystis* virus when they are placed into recently sterilized tanks filled with freshly made synthetic sea water. However, should they be placed in water which has recently housed perfectly healthy Indo-Pacific, Red Sea or central Pacific species, an epidemic of *Lymphocystis* disease will frequently result, even though the water is in perfect condition.

When juvenile, the Black Angelfish and the French Angelfish are extremely similar, both being blue-black with four vertical bars down the sides. However, the stripes of the Black Angelfish are somewhat lighter yellow than those of the French Angelfish. When adult, the Black Angelfish becomes a pewter-gray color with black dots on every scale. In a good specimen, filaments extend on the dorsal and anal fins almost to the posterior edge of the caudal fin.

French Angelfish *(Pomacanthus paru)*

The adult of this species is considerably smaller at 12 to 15 inches than the Black Angelfish at 18 to 22 inches. As previously stated, the vertical barring on the juvenile is a daffodil-yellow color, making it a much more attractive fish. It is also considerably more attractive as an adult, characterized by a charcoal-gray to black body color with the posterior margin of each scale having a creamy white to pale yellow edge. If anything, the French Angelfish is a little more fussy than the Black Angelfish with regard to feeding, although both species do well once settled into a suitably designed habitat.

72

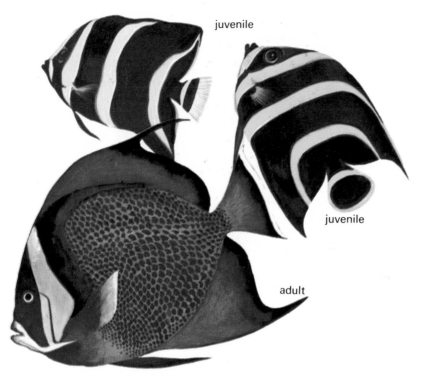

Juvenile forms of the Black and French Angelfishes are very
similar. Black Angelfish juvenile (*top left*) and adult (*above*),
and French Angelfish juvenile (*top right*) and young adult (*below*).

73

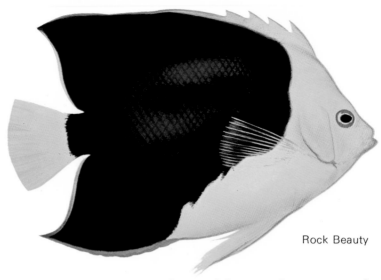

Rock Beauty

One cannot overstress the need for complete peace and quiet for a fish newly introduced into a marine aquarium. All too often, I am the recipient of agitated telephone calls from beginners asking why, despite the fact that they have offered ten different foods in the space of as many minutes, their newly purchased butterfly fish or angelfish is still cowering behind a rock. Nothing can be relied on more to send a nervous coral fish into a state of deep shock than this sort of behavior.

Rock Beauty *(Holocanthus tricolor)*
This splendid fish adorned in yellow, black and reddish-orange with a sapphire-blue eye is one of the toughest angelfishes from the Caribbean. I have kept several specimens of this slow-growing species for well over four years. Once adjusted to home aquarium life, they greedily accept all forms of food and, like the surgeonfishes, tangs and other marine angelfishes, they particularly relish the frequent inclusion of fresh spinach and chopped lettuce in their diet. Such green morsels must be introduced by the aquarist maintaining a tank under the clinical system. The algae growing naturally on the corals and rocks of the natural and seminatural system tanks will probably provide adequate greens without such supplements.

Queen Angelfish (*right*) and Blue Angelfish (*left*)

Queen and Blue Angelfish *(Holocanthus ciliarus, H. isabelita)*
There are obvious variations between the Queen Angelfish
and the Blue Angelfish. The hybrid of these two is Town-
send's Angelfish *(H. townsendi)*, but most taxonomists
accept only the two parent species as valid. The Queen
Angelfish is a breathtakingly beautiful animal which, again,
is restricted to the Caribbean area. Smaller specimens between 2 and 5 inches do well in the home aquarist's 25- to
80-gallon tanks, although to grow one of these creatures
to its full size of 12 to 18 inches, several years of care in a
150- to 200-gallon home aquarium would be needed. Like
all the angelfishes, the Queen Angelfish has a characteristic
razor-sharp curved spine on the base of each operculum
(gill cover). In the aquarium two fishes of the same sex
(or of different species) will raise their spines and wound
each other with vicious slashing movements if they feel that
their territory is being threatened. In the wild it is probable
that real fights result only from the most severe provocation,

but the aquarist must realize that his tank is not a full-sized coral reef and offers few places for the vanquished to retreat to safety. Generally speaking, one should never place two angelfishes together unless:
(1) they are at widely different stages of development as shown by their color patterns;
(2) the two fishes had been collected as a mated pair, or
(3) they are of different species.

Even if these conditions are met, the union should be attempted only if an adequate-sized reserve tank is available.

Checkered Angelfish *(Holocanthus xanthurus)*
This angelfish, like the Purple Moon Angelfish, is also strongly recommended for the beginner who wishes to try his hand at something a little more demanding than damselfishes. It comes mostly from the reefs around Ceylon, and will often commence feeding in the aquarium within 24 hours of its introduction.

As with almost all the more delicate reef fishes (i.e., butterfly fishes, surgeonfishes, tangs, sweetlips and wrasses), the angelfishes do not feel at all happy if placed into 100 percent fresh synthetic sea water. For this reason, it is much better to place them in an aquarium which has previously contained less demanding fishes for a month or so. This means that the water has had time to mature and that the gravel overlying the filter plate will contair a significant population of nitrifying bacteria, ensuring that both excreted ammonia and nitrites are rapidly and safely metabolized to harmless nitrates. If this is done, the newly introduced coral-reef fishes will never have to tolerate a dangerous concentration of toxic ammonia and nitrites. The exceptions to this rule are the Caribbean angelfishes previously mentioned. Because of their susceptibility to *Lymphocystis* viruses, it would be better to place them in a solution of one of the pre-aged synthetic salt formulae.

Majestic Angelfish *(Euxiphipops nevarchus)*
This glorious fish exhausts all superlatives. In prime condition it puts even the Emperor Angelfish to shame. Found on most of the reefs surrounding the Philippines, it is avail-

Checkered Angelfish (*above*) and Majestic Angelfish (*below*)

able only at a considerable cost, and large specimens are extremely expensive. Large public aquaria lucky enough to have a Majestic Angelfish on exhibition usually proudly display the fact in the entrance.

This is one of the more difficult marine fishes to persuade to start feeding in captivity and one must provide either well-matured sea water or a pre-aged preparation. However, even these precautions are not necessarily guarantors of success with this species.

Coral Beauty Angelfish *(Centropyge bispinosus)*
This pretty little angelfish extends over a wide area of the tropical shallow waters from East Africa to the Philippines and beyond. Its beauty is not as immediately striking as that of *Centropyge acanthops,* but it is nevertheless attractive. Both the Coral Beauty and the Purple Fireball will peacefully coexist in the same aquarium if adequate territory is provided for each of them.

Purple Fireball Angelfish *(Centropyge acanthops)*
Although having only two colors, deep purple and fiery orange, this small fish, adult at 2 to 2½ inches, is the cherished ward of a few lucky aquarists who maintain only a 20- to 30-gallon tank. It is a shy, secretive little creature, even after it has learned to associate its owner with food and security. A properly furnished aquarium for this species will take this fact into account and adequate provision for caves, rocky shelters and spatial coral intricacies should be made. This species may be restricted in range to the coral reefs of East Africa.

Centropyge argi
This attractive angelfish is not often seen and is believed to be quite rare throughout its range in the Caribbean, where it is only infrequently found at depths less than 100 feet. This species and the previous two fishes are sometimes known as dwarf angelfishes.

Coral Beauty Angelfish *(top)*. Purple Fireball Angelfish *(center)* and *Centropyge argi* *(bottom)*

79

Butterfly Fishes (Family Chaetodontidae)

Yellow Longnose Butterfly Fish *(Forcipiger longirostris)*

This fish has unjustly been labeled 'impossible' by several writers, some of whom appear never to have even attempted to keep it. The impression that this fish is difficult to keep is undoubtedly conveyed by the enormous lengthening of the upper and lower jaw. This is an adaptation to facilitate the removal of small mollusks and crustaceans from within coral heads and would suggest that the fish is a finicky feeder. However, this fish is so tough and adaptable in captivity that it will accept all manner of the usual aquarium foods within a few days of introduction to a tank. The Yellow Longnose is at least as tough and hardy as another much maligned butterfly fish, the Copper Band Butterfly Fish, but it takes to aquarium feeding much more readily.

A fish of this species in good condition illustrates why the common name for the family is butterfly fishes. Many people have watched or collected butterflies when young and are familiar with the insects' resting stance with both wings touching and in the vertical plane. The butterfly fishes are all compressed laterally, and consequently they resemble butterflies in the resting position in shape and often in markings. The slightly spasmodic movements of these fishes when searching for food among rocks and corals is also not

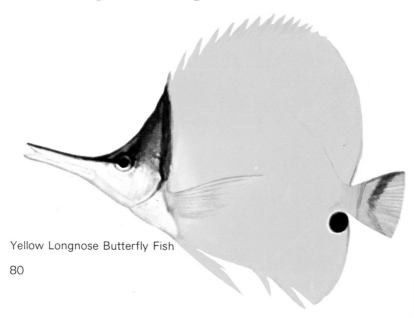

Yellow Longnose Butterfly Fish

unlike the fluttering of butterflies.

The Yellow Longnose Butterfly Fish is strongly recommended to anyone who feels that he has the confidence and, preferably, the experience to tackle this family, which includes some of the truly 'impossibles', such as the Rainbow Butterfly Fish. This impressive fish is the despair of even the most experienced aquarists because of its refusal to eat anything other than the polyps of living corals.

Copper Band Butterfly Fish *(Chelmon rostratus)*

Apart from the obvious differences in coloration, this fish strongly resembles the Yellow Longnose in shape, although the jaws are slightly less elongated in relation to the body size.

The Copper Band Butterfly Fish may be difficult to encourage to start feeding in captivity. This is particularly true of those specimens originating from the Singapore area rather than those imported from the Philippines. However, provided that conditions in the aquarium are excellent with regard to correct physical (lighting, specific gravity, temperature and so on), chemical (*p*H, low toxin content and so on) and psychological (adequate cover, absence of aggressors and so on) parameters, this lovely fish will nearly always be tempted with slivers of fresh mussel mantle or squid. From then on, it will always feed.

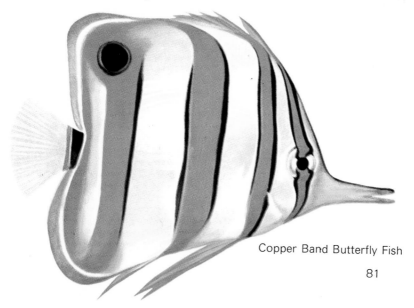

Copper Band Butterfly Fish

Wimplefish

Wimplefish *(Heniochus acuminatus)*
This butterfly fish is distinct from the other members of its
family, having lengthened rays of the dorsal fin and a generally high body. It is strikingly adorned with black stripes
on a silver background. Wimplefishes seldom present any difficulties with regard to feeding. They readily accept all foods,
including dried flake offerings and freeze-dried products.

Although there are several species within this genus, including *H. permutatus, H. singularis* and *H. cornutus,* the
Wimplefish is the commonest, cheapest, hardiest and, in my
opinion, the prettiest member of the genus. An extremely
successful reef fish, it is circumtropical in distribution from
the reefs of tropical East Africa through to the far eastern
atolls of the central Pacific and shows remarkably little variation throughout its range.

When juvenile, Wimplefishes, like some other members

82

of the family Chaetodontidae, will often be seen swimming up to other much larger fishes, and starting to peck away at their flanks, heads, fins and gills. It is presumed that these juveniles are fulfilling the same function as the Cleaner Wrasse *(Labroides dimidiatus)* in ridding the larger fishes of troublesome ectoparasites. As a result of a certain similarity in external appearances, the Wimplefish is sometimes mistaken for the Moorish Idol *(Zanclus cornutus)*, although the two fishes are not even distantly related.

Golden Butterfly Fish *(Chaetodon auriga)*
This fish is probably the most successful within its genus in terms of numerical superiority. Its range is identical to that of the Wimplefish, but the sheer weight of numbers in the areas in which it is found indicate that it is a remarkable colonizer. It is sometimes known as the Threadfin Butterfly Fish. In view of its ubiquity, one might expect the connoisseur of marine animals to be uninterested in it. However, it is popular with even marine aquarists of long standing.

Although a common and hardy butterfly fish, this species is by no means the hardiest in captivity. That honor falls to the Sunburst Butterfly Fish—the ideal species for the beginner.

Golden Butterfly Fish

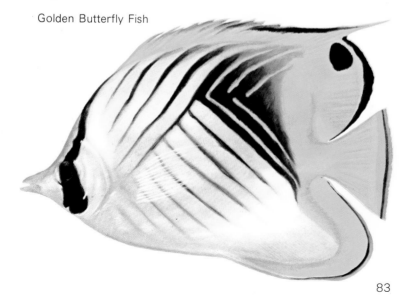

Black-wedge Butterfly Fish *(Chaetodon falcula)*

This butterfly fish also has a wide range from the Indo-Pacific through to the central Pacific, but it is not numerous anywhere. It is also known as the Saddled Butterfly Fish. It is certainly not among the easiest butterfly fishes to begin feeding in the aquarium. However, like the Copper Band, once feeding has begun in earnest, the Black-wedge Butterfly Fish proves to be one of the most indestructible of all the marine aquarium occupants.

Unlike the Golden, Moon and Sunburst Butterfly Fishes, this fish is seldom obtainable in small sizes. Most specimens seen offered for sale are young adults measuring around 3 to 4 inches in body length. This may well account for the difficulties often experienced in getting the Black-wedge to feed in captivity. It is not unlikely that an adult fish would have already formed very definite feeding habits and preferences for certain items of diet not available in the marine aquarium. Modifying such established habits might prove more difficult for an older fish than for a relatively young one.

Moon Butterfly Fish *(Chaetodon lunula)*

After the Sunburst Butterfly Fish, this fish is possibly the next most trouble-free member of its genus. After several months' study of the special requirements of the most difficult family to coral-reef fishes to culture successfully in the home marine aquarium, the novice may feel competent enough to try his new-found skills on either of these two fishes. The Moon Butterfly Fish has the same wide range as *C. auriga* and *C. falcula.*

In the marine aquarium, the Moon Butterfly Fish soon settles down and apparently loses all fear of its owner. The olive-green body color is unusual among coral-reef fishes and unique among butterfly fishes.

Butterfly fishes are not especially aggressive toward other coral-reef fishes except members of the same sex and species, although in an overcrowded tank some threat display may be seen. This almost always takes the form of head-down circling movements with all fins extended. The needle-sharp points of the dorsal fin rays are stiffly erected, and short forward-thrusting movements generally suffice to deter transgressors from any further antagonism.

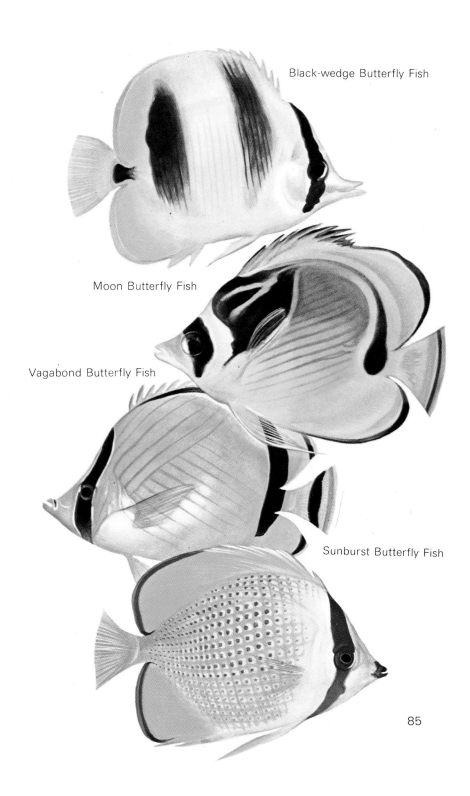

Black-wedge Butterfly Fish

Moon Butterfly Fish

Vagabond Butterfly Fish

Sunburst Butterfly Fish

Vagabond Butterfly Fish *(Chaetodon vagabundus)*

This fish, which is also known as the Criss Cross Butterfly Fish, like the very similar C. *pictus*, does not do particularly well in the home aquarium, although, as with all rules, there will always be notable exceptions. The main reason for illustrating the fish here is to warn all except very experienced aquarists from including this fish in their collection. The principal problem that is experienced is its refusal to feed adequately and consistently in the marine aquarium. In consequence, the nutrients it gleans from its finicky picking among the corals, rocks and gravel hardly seem to supply the requirements of its *basal metabolism* (the basic minimum chemical activity of an organism necessary for the maintenance of the life processes).

Sunburst Butterfly Fish *(Chaetodon kleini)*

The flanks of this fish have an attractive golden coloration, each scale being marked with a darkish spot. These spots appear to be blue-black under normal top lighting, but when the fish is seen under reflected front light, it will be noticed that both the spots and the vertical head stripes are a rich purple-blue color.

This fish is unique among the family Chaetodontidae for its hardiness, resistance to disease and eagerness to feed in captivity. It is sometimes known as the White-spotted Butterfly Fish. Of the butterfly fishes, this species is probably the easiest to keep.

Brown Butterfly Fish *(Chaetodon collare)*

Almost all fishes of this species offered for sale come from the reefs and shallow waters surrounding India, Pakistan and Ceylon. The beginner has already been advised not to purchase specimens of this species. A significant proportion of those fishes I have attempted to culture have not responded to even the most painstaking efforts.

The Brown Butterfly Fish is included here because its coloration, an unusual purple-brown, is rare among coral fishes. Also, because it is a difficult subject, it constitutes the sort of challenge that the advanced marine aquarist may care to take up one day.

Brown Butterfly Fish

Rainbow Butterfly Fish

Rainbow Butterfly Fish *(Chaetodon trifasciatus)*
This species, also known as the Lineated Butterfly Fish, is probably the most beautiful fish in the whole genus. Unfortunately, however, it is also the most exasperating, for it frequently refuses all normal foods offered to it in captivity. The following notes may be of use to aquarists attempting to keep this difficult fish for the first time.

First, a large specimen should be obtained (i.e., between 3 and 4 inches). A butterfly fish of any species which is 'narrow' behind the head should never be bought. Second, a large, approximately 80-gallon aquarium should be used with pre-aged synthetic sea water and a great deal of rockwork and coral formations. Feeding should start with live coral heads, followed by half-grown brine shrimp larvae and, after a few weeks, the fishes should be weaned on to vitamin-soaked, freeze-dried brine shrimps.

Addis Butterfly Fish *(Chaetodon semilarvatus)*
This richly colored species comes only from the Red Sea, and its distinctive coloration and markings make it easy to spot even in films such as those made by Jacques Cousteau. A specimen in prime condition will always show several orange-yellow bars on the flanks and the rust-colored eye spot.

If this butterfly fish is kept at the normal temperature of 75° to 80°F (24° to 26°C), its basal metabolism appears to proceed at a very slow rate. This is probably due to the fact that this species comes from the lukewarm waters of the Red Sea and has therefore evolved a body chemistry capable of withstanding the losses due to high saline content and high water temperature. I had one exceptionally recalcitrant specimen which for a time refused all foods. During this period there was no noticeable decline in activity or reduction in weight. One day it suddenly accepted prawn eggs and has fed greedily ever since. It has lived for almost two years in captivity, though it was clearly an adult, measuring 5 inches, when imported.

The significance of this experience, which has often been repeated with this species, is that any other butterfly fish, with its high basal metabolic rate, would have wasted

Addis Butterfly Fish

Four-eyed Butterfly Fish

89

away without food in 15 to 20 days. Individuals in captivity show considerable variation in habits and needs. One specimen may accept every food offered, including dried foods, whereas another will refuse all but small pieces of fresh protein. With all butterfly fishes it will be found that regular (twice weekly) feedings with a properly formulated vitamin complex available from marine and pet stores will be of invaluable assistance in keeping the fish in as good condition as, or occasionally in better condition than, when it lived on the reef. On the reef it was subject to predation by groupers, sharks, barracudas and moray eels and had to compete with many other reef animals for the available foods. Probably the easiest way of adding such a vitamin preparation to a food is to dissolve the crystalline vitamin mixture in a little tap water and then soak freeze-dried pieces of brine shrimp in the solution for 24 hours in the refrigerator. The resulting food must be kept in the refrigerator at all times since once added to water and allowed to attain room temperature, many of the vitamins are prone to swift oxidation.

Four-eyed Butterfly Fish *(Chaetodon capistratus)*
This fish is found only in the Caribbean area. Although it has often been reported to be hardy in captivity, it does not compare in this respect with the Sunburst Butterfly Fish. The black spot and the disruptive dark bar through the eye probably cause predators to mistake the back end for the front.

General hints for the care of butterfly fishes
(1) These coral-reef fishes are very prone to shock if mishandled at any time during their transfer to the home aquarium. The styrofoam-lined box in which the fishes are transferred home *must not* be suddenly opened in a brilliantly lit room. If it is daytime, the curtains should be drawn. If in the evening, the room lights should be extinguished with the exception of a low-wattage table lamp. Also, the aquarium lights should be off, and should be left off until the following day.
(2) Established fishes in the aquarium should be well fed prior to the introduction of the new fishes.
(3) Butterfly fishes should never be placed in sea water with even a trace of nitrite or ammonia contamination. If this

advice is ignored, it is certain that even if the narcotic effect of these toxins is not immediately fatal, the general weakening effect they will have on the fishes will so lower their natural resistance to disease that they will quickly succumb to a multiple infection and die.

(4) Butterfly fishes smaller than 2 inches should never be purchased. Infant fishes this size need to feed on planktonic life-forms and coral polyps almost continually for 12 hours per day. Unless the aquarist has unlimited time, patience and brine shrimp hatching facilities, it is unlikely that he will be successful in raising young fishes.

(5) When choosing a butterfly fish from a dealer's tank, always look for the following characteristics:

(a) The fish should possess the light coloration typical for the species. Any darker than normal fishes should be viewed with suspicion.

(b) The respiratory rate, indicated by the frequency of the gill cover movements, should be around 80 to 100 movements per minute, assuming that the water temperature is normal at 75° to 80°F (24° to 26°C), and that aeration and filtration are adequate.

(c) A healthy fish will not swim with the pelvic fins permanently clamped to its belly, but will from time to time lower them and swim for several seconds with them extended. (This is also a guide for indicating the state of health of the closely related angelfishes).

(d) If possible, always try to witness the butterfly fish feeding on foods you can procure before making a purchase.

(e) A fish that is active and displays an inquisitive interest in its environment is usually a sounder fish than one which is shy and retiring.

(f) No matter what the state of health of the fish, do not buy either the Rainbow or Brown Butterfly Fish. Fishes of these species, together with C. larvatus and C. octofasciatus, are best left to the very wealthy and/or skillful, and certainly should never be bought by beginners.

One final tip can be given for butterfly fishes reluctant to feed. Few can resist a juicy live coral head and although such a delicacy is expensive, it is sometimes worthwhile to persuade an expensive fish to feed.

91

Surgeonfishes and tangs (Family Acanthuridae)
Emperor Tang *(Zebrasoma xanthurum)*

All the fishes in the surgeon and tang family are so called because of the existence of razor-sharp 'scalpels' tucked into hollow sheaths at the base of the tail. When angry or afraid, the fish can raise these devices at right angles to the body and, as a result of a threshing action of the tail, inflict terrible wounds on the body or fins of an adversary. These fishes will not hesitate to inflict the same sort of treatment on a human hand, so the greatest possible care must be exercised if handling a member of this group.

Like all the members of this family, Emperor Tangs have a great liking for greens in their diet. Three or four times each week, these fishes should receive a good feeding of freshly thawed frozen spinach, or better still, fresh spinach. Such vegetation does not, of course, exist in the fishes' natural environment, so most coral-reef fishes have to be taught to eat it. This is best achieved by allowing the fishes to fast for a whole day. Then, on the first feeding of the following day, spinach (or even chopped lettuce) should be offered. Usually the fishes will be so hungry that they will swallow the proffered food without realizing what they have eaten, and an increasingly strong liking is usually developed for this valuable food. All the surgeonfishes and tangs are swift and powerful swimmers and have a real need for large open spaces within the aquarium.

Yellow-green Striped Surgeonfish *(Acanthurus lineatus)*

This fish ranks with another member of its genus, the Majestic Surgeonfish, as one of the most pleasingly shaped and graceful movers on the reef. Its range is circumtropical in shallow seas and on reefs, but it is absent from the tropical Atlantic. This surgeonfish is a most undemanding species to feed, and will readily take all the usual aquarium foods.

Powder-blue Surgeonfish *(Acanthurus leucosternon)*

The novice aquarist is advised not to attempt to keep this species until he has had several months' experience with less difficult members of the genus.

Powder-blue Surgeonfishes do not have a wide range and

Emperor Tang

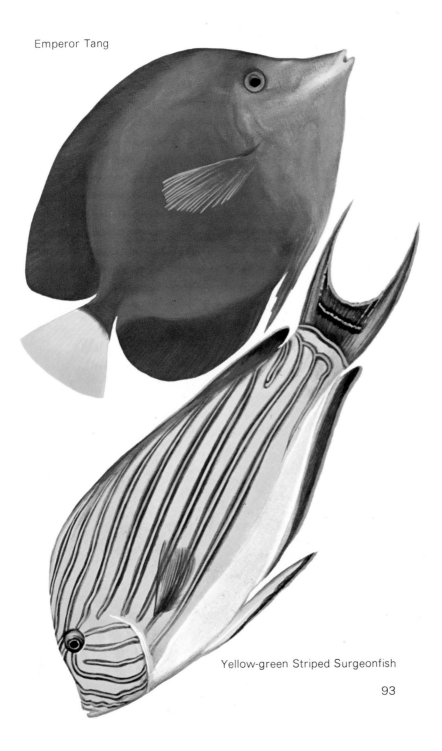

Yellow-green Striped Surgeonfish

93

Powder-blue Surgeonfish

Majestic Surgeonfish

are most common in the Indo-Pacific. The species travels badly; therefore, when selecting a specimen, greater than normal care should be taken to insure that the fish is completely unmarked. In addition, the areas around the head and chest should be an enamel-white color and any fish that is a dirty gray or off-white color in this region should not be purchased. The dorsal fin of a healthy Powder-blue Surgeonfish will usually be slightly erected; a fin clamped to the body indicates disease and a stiffly erected fin shows that the fish has recently been badly shocked.

The abnormal length of the intestine of this species indicates that it is primarily herbivorous in the wild. In the sea aquarium, however, a healthy specimen will soon learn to eat live foods and even fresh protein. Vitamin-soaked brine shrimp is an excellent 'starter' for the species.

Majestic Surgeonfish (Acanthurus sohal)

This species is restricted in its distribution to the Red Sea area, where it is never common, making it a fairly expensive fish to buy. It is sometimes known as the Striped Surgeonfish. It is not only one of the most graceful and beautifully colored of the coral-reef fishes, but it is also undoubtedly one of the most undemanding. Its advantages are weakened only by the fact that many specimens become increasingly intolerant of certain other species as they reach the three- to four-year-old stage. A three-year-old Majestic Surgeonfish I own has recently destroyed an adult batfish (Platax teira) and an adult Bluering Angelfish. Both of the attacked fishes were large and powerful and had lived with the surgeonfish for the previous two years. The fishes were killed during the night and were found the following morning covered with wounds from the sharp 'scalpels' of the surgeonfish.

Regal Tang (Paracanthurus hepatus)

The Regal Tang, or Flagtail Surgeonfish, has been described as 'the bluest thing on earth'. This tang is ideally suited to the smaller marine aquarium, since it reaches an adult length of only about 4 inches. It is probably a schooling fish on the Philippino reefs, the home of most specimens, and so does not object to the company of members of its own species.

95

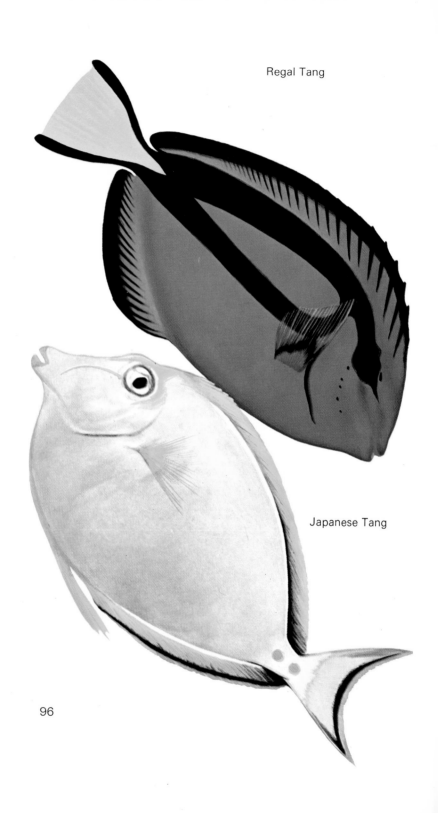

Regal Tang

Japanese Tang

96

Even a small marine aquarium of 36 inches x 18 inches x 18 inches (i.e., 40 gallons) can safely house two or three specimens at 1½ to 2 inches.

After its introduction to the aquarium, the Regal Tang usually goes into a state of mild shock and will frequently terrify its new owner by lying flat on the gravel under a stone or coral head, or leaning against the side of the tank. However, provided that the overanxious aquarist can desist from prodding and poking the frightened fish, and assuming that the water is in good condition without even a trace of nitrite content, the hardy little fellow will always rally.

Japanese Tang *(Naso lituratus)*
I have not been able to discover whether this colorful species is very common in Japanese waters, but it is not common anywhere throughout the remainder of its range in the Indo- and central Pacific.

The 'scalpel' device of the surgeons in this tang is modified to form two bony extensions that are permanently erected in the mature fish. As a result of this feature, any movement of this species from one tank to another should always be made using a special type of net made by sewing a plastic bag onto a normal net frame and then cutting holes in the bag for drainage. If a nylon or cotton net is used, the opercular spines will become entangled in the net, causing serious damage to the fish.

The Japanese Tang has a real need for considerable amounts of vegetable matter in its diet, although like most marine herbivores it soon acquires omnivorous habits.

Sailfin Tang *(Zebrasoma veliferum)*
Remarkable variation occurs in coloration of this species over its range. Indo-Pacific specimens have a complicated coloration, whereas those from the central Pacific (the East Indies) have the simpler black and white alternate barring. The Indo-Pacific race is generally tougher than the race from the central Pacific, although the latter is hardy and specimens will live for well over three years if purchased as young 2- or 3-inch fishes.

Large specimens of this species become very active in the

early evening, a period that in the wild probably coincides with the heaviest feeding of the day. It would thus be cruel to house a Sailfin Tang, or any other semipelagic species, in an aquarium which was not at least twelve times longer and three times wider than the overall length of the fish. This means that a good-sized specimen should be housed in a tank at least 6 feet long and 18 inches wide and between 18 to 24 inches in depth. Smaller specimens with a total length of 2 to 3 inches could be housed in the popular-sized 36-inch x 12-inch x 15-inch marine aquarium, where they would probably remain dwarfed throughout their lives. The mechanism by which the ultimate size of a fish is closely related to the size of the aquarium in which it is housed is imperfectly understood and should form the subject of a serious study. One theory is that when the concentration of some of the fish's waste products reaches a certain level, these products begin to act as growth inhibitors. This may well be partly correct since the growth of certain fishes (in particular the dragonfishes) will recommence as a result of regular freshwater changes.

Sailfin Tang
Indo-Pacific form

98

Moorish Idols (Family Zanclidae)
Moorish Idol *(Zanclus canescens)*

The Moorish Idol is paradoxically probably the most photographed but least understood coral-reef fish kept in the marine aquarium. Its bizarre shape and striking coloration have always attracted the attention of the artist and photographer, and it is consequently the tropical marine fish best known to the general public. It has an extensive Pacific range, being found off Zanzibar and Mauritius, throughout the Indian Ocean and as far east as offshore Mexico.

Although it seems to have a superficial resemblance to the Wimplefish, it is difficult to imagine two fishes which are more different. Whereas the Wimplefish will eat almost any foods offered, the Moorish Idol frequently drives its owner to distraction by refusing even the most tasty tidbits. The Wimplefish usually remains free of disease in captivity, whereas the Moorish Idol will fall victim to a variety of pathogenic bacteria, protozoa and viruses.

An aquarist of my acquaintance, determined to be the first to succeed with this difficult species, heard from a merchant sailor that he had seen large shoals of Moorish Idols feeding unperturbably on ships' waste in the waters of a Philippino dockyard. Reasoning that the missing ingredient for this species was good, old-fashioned filth, he placed two ounces of raw steak into his aquarium and left it to rot. Thirty-six hours later, he had not only killed his Moorish Idol but had prematurely terminated the lives of six other previously healthy and happy fishes. If the aquarist had paused to consider the problem, he would have realized that even were the sailor's doubtful story accurate, the fishes, presumably driven into the harbor waters by the lack of a certain food on the reef, could simply turn around and swim back out to the clear waters of the reef as soon as they had had enough of the filthy harbor water—a possibility denied the aquarist's fishes. With regard to the authenticity of the sailor's story, I once watched a group of 18 to 20 adult Moorish Idols every afternoon for nearly a month in the Indian Ocean. They refused to swim any nearer than 200 yards to the place where a stream used as an open sewer by a native village emptied into the sea.

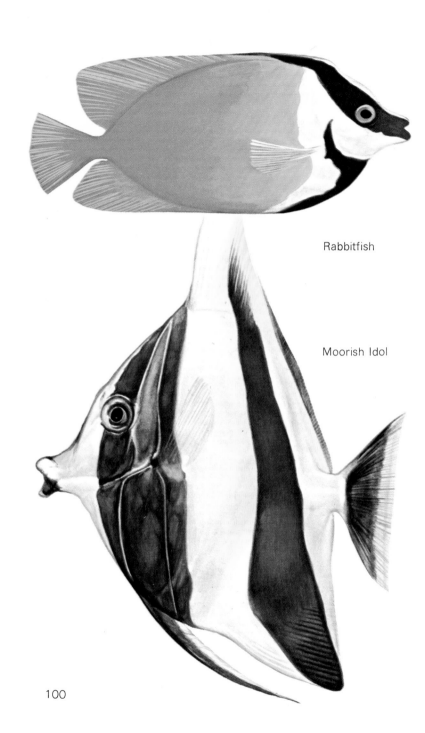

Rabbitfish

Moorish Idol

100

Rabbitfishes (Family Siganidae)
Rabbitfish *(Lo vulpinus)*
This close relative of the Moorish Idol is sometimes called the Badgerfish because of the patterning in black and white around the head. It never seems to have enjoyed great popularity. The species has a limited range in the Pacific Ocean, being common only around the Philippines. Although a shy species, it feeds exceptionally well in captivity. An oddity is that at eight- to ten-day intervals it sheds its mucous body coat and secretes another one.

Snappers (Family Lutianidae)
Arabian Snapper *(Lutianus kasmira)*
Only two species of this genus have been included here, though not because these fishes are especially difficult to keep. On the contrary, in common with damselfishes, any of the snappers may be confidently recommended to the beginner.

The Arabian Snapper, or Blue-banded Sea Perch, is often obtainable at juvenile sizes of 1½ to 2½ inches. At these sizes it is quite manageable, but is a gluttonous feeder. If the aquarist could spare the time, feeding these fishes on the

Arabian Snapper

hour every hour would be most acceptable to them. When they smell the presence of food in the water or optimistically observe the approach of their keeper, a wild form of behavior similar to that of a shark 'frenzy' invariably results. Should the aquarium house several of these fishes, the surface of the water appears to 'boil' with their greedy, mad threshings.

As these fishes become increasingly boisterous with growth, it would be wise to house them only with fishes of phlegmatic constitutions such as triggerfishes, dragonfishes (*Pterois* spp and others) and groupers.

Emperor Snapper *(Lutianus sebae)*
This is a most distinctive species in coloration, markings and body shape. The Emperor, or Red, Snapper is characterized by the same gross feeding habits as the preceding member of the genus, but very quickly grows to a much larger size. Exceptional specimens up to 30 inches in length are occasionally taken by anglers off East Africa. It is

Emperor Snapper

not common anywhere, but the species does have a wide range throughout the Pacific and Indian Oceans. Only the juveniles, which are usually sooty black and white, are found in shallow reef waters, the adults usually moving in groups over deeper water.

An unusual feature of this fish is that, as it grows older, the darker bars lighten from black, through dark brown to reddish-brown, until at maturity the fish is a rich mahogany-red color. When excited, a flush of salmon-pink hue spreads into the white areas.

Grunts and sweetlips (Family Plectorhynchidae)
Polka-dot Grunt *(Plectorhynchus chaetodonoides)*
At present, this fish ranks with those species mentioned in this book as being unsuitable as culture subjects for all except the wealthy and the dedicated researcher. However, I have no doubt whatsoever that this and other species which now require the skills and resources of the specialist will

Polka-dot Grunt

eventually be as simple to keep as damselfishes. Within the next few years enormous advances in techniques and materials should be made by today's novices.

The major problem with the Polka-dot Grunt, as with all other contemporary 'impossible' marine fishes, is that of getting the fish to feed substantially in the marine aquarium. The fishes need to derive enough energy from food, not only to replace energy expended in maintaining the basal metabolic processes (i.e., digestion, respiration, osmo-regulation and others), but also to maintain sufficient reserves to repair damage to the body and, if the animal is juvenile, to promote growth. It is not enough for the fish to pick here and there in a desultory fashion.

The range of this grunt is from Malaysia to the most eastern coral islands of the eastern Pacific.

Spotted Sweetlips *(Plectorhynchus orientalis)*
Although this attractive fish is related to the previous species, it is exceptionally hardy and eager to feed in captivity. In larger tanks it may quickly reach a size in excess of that which the owner originally expected. Thirty-inch specimens may occasionally be seen in public aquaria.

Damselfishes (Family Pomacentridae)
Green Forktail Damselfish *(Chromis cyanea)*
It has been mentioned more than once so far that the damselfishes, or demoisellefishes, are ideal species for the beginner. Unfortunately, however, it is inadvisable to include more than one member of each species in an aquarium of less than a 60-gallon capacity, unless one has been lucky enough to obtain a definite male and female pair.

The Green Forktail Damselfish (sometimes called the Blue Chromis) is the exception to the rule and, like the common Mediterranean Brown Forktail Damselfish *(Chromis chromis),* it is naturally a schooling fish. This means that even in a small, 30-gallon marine aquarium, half a dozen or so of these iridescent blue-green beauties may be kept together without too much fighting.

On the reef, a large school of 50 or so adults will face into a prevailing current and periodically dart forward to capture

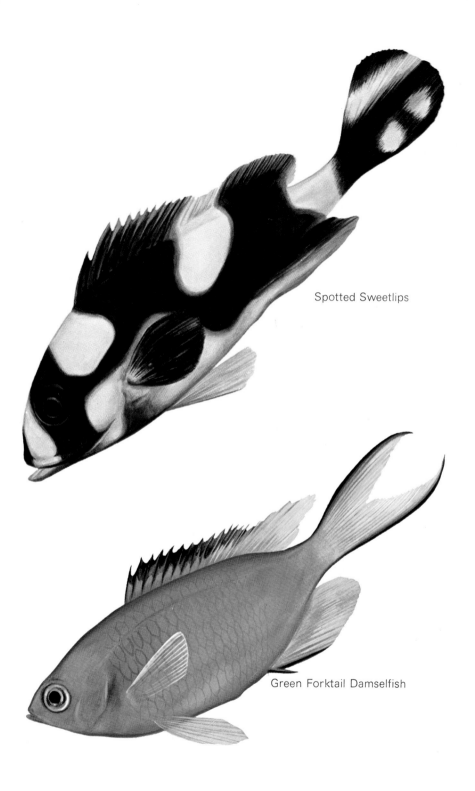

Spotted Sweetlips

Green Forktail Damselfish

some planktonic morsel of food. In the home aquarium these pretty fishes quickly settle down to a varied and undemanding diet of dried food, chopped earthworm, prawn flesh, chopped heart or steak and whiteworm.

Sergeant Major *(Abudefduf saxatalis)*
The Sergeant Major has a truly circumtropical distribution, being almost as common on the reefs of the tropical Atlantic as it is in the Pacific, Indo-Pacific and Red Sea, where it lives in small communities. The amazing hardiness of this fish has to be experienced to be believed. On my last collecting trip to the Indian Ocean, I brought back to Zambia a collection of reef fishes which included two Sergeant Majors. When the time came to dispose of equipment and animals among fellow aquarists, the marine fishes could not be placed because of the then-current lack of marine experience and interest among aquarists. A Dutch friend finally agreed to accept them but I later learned that, quickly tiring of their aggressive behavior and lack of bright colors, he had disposed of them by dropping them into a brine shrimp hatching tank, containing only cooking salt solution—but nine months later they were still alive and thriving!

Sergeant Major

Humbug Damselfish

Humbug Damselfish *(Dascyllus aruanus)*
The Humbug Dameselfish is one of the most aggressive members of a family noted for aggression. Its sense of territorial ownership is well developed and makes life particularly difficult for the importer who, because of the popularity of the species as an inexpensive, attractive beginner's fish, must always carry large stocks. In a tank between 60 and 80 gallons or larger, a small 'family' of six to eight of these fishes will quickly settle in, each one taking up station in its allotted territory which it only really leaves to chase off an intruder or to snap up food. These fishes are prized for their alertness and smart appearance, hardiness, low cost and aesthetic value in complementing the more obvious impact made by larger fishes, but Humbug Damselfishes also have a definite ecological niche to fill in the marine aquarium. At meal times they reduce the dangers of organic pollution by catching scraps of food that would otherwise go unnoticed by the bigger fishes. They will survive dangerously high nitrite levels, eat anything remotely edible, tolerate temperatures from 70° to 85° F and, with the minimum of effort on the part of the aquarist, survive in almost any

concentration of unsatisfactory artificial seawater formulae. As such, they are most invaluable to the beginner since, forgiving the mistakes he will probably make, they will survive. The Humbug Damselfish is found in all shallow seas in the tropics except the tropical Atlantic.

Cloudy Damselfish *(Dascyllus reticulatus)*
This is an exceptionally pretty fish whose colors are very much understated. The Cloudy Damselfish is found throughout the tropical Indo-Pacific region although only in Ceylonese waters is it as common as the Domino Damselfish.

Domino Damselfish *(Dascyllus trimaculatus)*
When juvenile or newly imported, this species, which is also sometimes called the Three-spotted Damselfish, is a deep sooty-black all over with little or no trace of iridescence. As it matures in captivity, the intensity of the blackness may decline somewhat so that it becomes a dark, metallic-gray color. It is now believed that this change is due to some deficiency in captivity since 3- to 4-inch specimens can be seen still showing total melanism though obviously adult.

Cloudy Damselfish

Recent work has shown that a diet rich in vitamin D will correct this loss of color.

The Domino Damselfish is very territorial in behavior, and will often show its displeasure at the violation of its spatial possessions by rapidly oscillating up and down in the water, somewhat resembling a yo-yo on an invisible string. It has other ways of expressing anger and resentment. The marine aquarist may be suddenly aware of a deep, throaty, porcine grunting noise in a room whose pig population is conspicuously nonexistent. Initial feelings of alarm will usually be replaced by amusement on discovering that this surprisingly audible noise issues from the damselfishes in the marine aquarium.

I have witnessed one spawning of Domino Damselfishes once and two spawnings of Cloudy Damselfishes in my 80-gallon aquaria. On each occasion, the mode of reproduction was noticeably similar to that of the Cichlidae, a freshwater family of fishes. An initial courtship display consisting of face-to-face slow circling, accompanied by much fin quivering and body shaking, takes from 20 to 90 minutes to com-

Domino Damselfish

109

plete. Then the female, from whose vent a short, blunt, white ovipositor tube protrudes, proceeds to deposit a string of large (0.75 mm in diameter) fawn-colored eggs on a stone, shell or coral surface. Having completed a row of five to twelve eggs, she retires and the male, who has meanwhile been defending the spawning site from all intruders, now moves in and sprays the eggs with milt. This procedure is repeated until the female is exhausted of eggs. The eggs in my aquaria were left with the parents, but the fry were unfortunately eaten either by the parent fishes or by other fishes in the tank.

Black Velvet Damselfish *(Abudefduf oxydon)*
It is difficult to believe that this gorgeous creature is related to the Sergeant Major. It is the most magnificent fish in the damselfish group. Because it is rare in the Philippines where most specimens originate, it is always expensive.

Saffron-blue Damselfish *(Pomacentrus melanochir)*
This species is sometimes also called the Yellow-tailed Damselfish. The coloring of this species is simple, with a radiant blue body and a yellow tail, but the overall effect is most spectacular. Many Saffron-blue Damselfishes come originally from the reefs around Ceylon, where the fish is quite common.

Black Velvet Damselfish

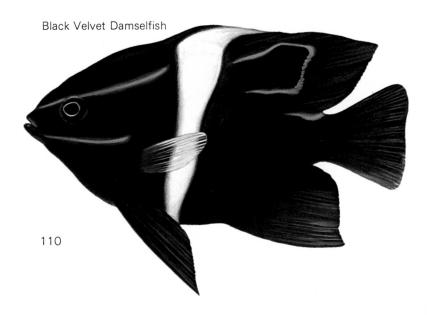

110

Saffron-blue Damselfish

When buying these fishes for the small home marine aquarium, buy either only one of each species or, with a larger tank, nine to twelve of each species. If only two are purchased (even if the fishes are a male and female pair) apart from the spawning season when they will just tolerate each other, there will be incessant bickering and fighting between them. Strangely enough, when a relatively large number of the same species are housed in the same tank, very little real aggression occurs, although there will still be occasional threatening behavior. The probable explanation for this is that in large numbers each fish becomes slightly bewildered as to which of its fellow residents it should attack first; in consequence, it seldom attacks any of them.

Electric-blue Damselfish *(Pomacentrus caeruleus)*
This species is very common around the Philippine group of islands. It is as aggressive as any other of the damsel family, so when stocking average-sized aquaria, the rule will again be only one per tank.

Many of the damselfishes show a marked preference for demolition and excavation work, and perhaps in no other member of the family are these talents more highly developed than in the Electric-blue Damselfish. Many a marine aquarist

Electric-blue Damselfish

with a flair for decor in the arrangement of his corals, rocks, shells and gravel has seen his artistic creation slowly but resolutely redesigned by a small damselfish. However, tolerance is a small price to pay for the pleasure and amusement afforded by such a beautiful creature. As with all damselfishes, anything and everything is eaten with great relish.

Clownfishes (Family Pomacentridae)
Common Clownfish (Amphiprion percula)
The Common Clownfish, or Orange Anemone Fish, is always popular because of its availability, good color, relative hardiness and low cost. It is priced comparatively low by collectors in Singapore and the Philippines, so it is probably a very common and easily caught fish in those areas.

This species is familiar in public aquaria, dealers' shops and the home aquarium and has probably been as responsible as the Moorish Idol and the seahorse for many 'converts' to the pleasures of marine-keeping. In no other species is the most typical coral-reef fish feature, the sudden division between two adjoining colors, so highly developed.

These fishes are among the most sociable of all coral-reef fishes, and many of them may be kept in one aquarium with

112

a minimum of fighting. They like a high temperature, between 78° and 80° F, and will thrive on almost any foods available. This accommodating tendency should not be abused, however. A meal two or three times weekly of fresh protein (chopped liver, steak, prawn or squid) or, even better, live food such as chopped earthworm, will greatly enhance their color and general condition.

It is fascinating to see these fishes nestling down among the tentacles of a sea anemone. The members of the genus *Amphiprion* have, without exception, evolved a *symbiotic* union with anemones of the *Stoichactis* genus and, ideally, should always be kept with an anemone. (A symbiotic union is a relationship between two organisms in which both parties directly benefit from the arrangement). The thousands of nematocysts (stinging cells) on each tentacle would paralyze and kill the clownfish if they were fired. However, the anemone, benefiting as it does from food brought to it by the clownfish, never fires off the nematocysts at the fish after an initial introductory period, and thus protects it from attacks by other fishes that would be promptly stung to death if they were foolhardy enough to pursue the clownfish into the anemone's deadly embrace.

Common Clownfish

Red Clownfish *(Amphiprion frenatus)*

The Red Clownfish or Red Anemone Fish is found throughout the tropical western Pacific, from Singapore to southern Japan. Specimens from Singapore may be a dark chocolate-brown color on the body, whereas most from the Philippines are a glowing orange-red. This fish is aggressive toward its own species and only one should be kept per tank, unless the aquarist is lucky enough to obtain a mated pair—a bond which incidentally appears to be permanent.

Black Clownfish *(Amphiprion sebae)*

This fish, like the Red Clownfish, may tolerate others of its species when young, but as it approaches sexual maturity at 1¼ to 2 inches it becomes intolerant of all but its mate. It too seems to form a permanent partnership, so that if the

Red Clownfish

aquarist can obtain a mated pair, an interesting aquarium can be created with no other life-forms but a large *Stoichactis* anemone and the two fishes. If fed well on fresh, live protein, the pair will usually spawn. A pair I kept in a 70-gallon aquarium spawned eight times at 20-day intervals between August and December 1969. The eggs were zealously guarded by both parents during the development period when they were attached to a flat stone. As soon as they hatched, however, invariably at three to five o'clock in the morning, the parents ate them before they could be removed.

Chocolate Clownfish *(Amphiprion xanthurus)*
There is a large group of clownfishes, including *A. xanthurus, A. polymnurus* and *A. bicintus,* which may well prove to be variations of a single species in the same way that

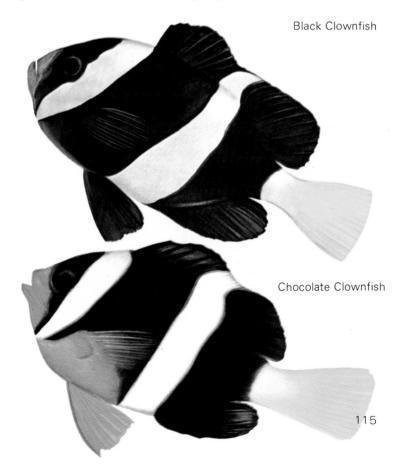

Black Clownfish

Chocolate Clownfish

115

all batfishes may belong to the same species, with major geographic variations in color and form. The Chocolate Clownfish is fairly common throughout the Indian Ocean and the whole tropical Pacific area. It begins to exhibit aggression to others of the species as it matures.

Teak Clownfish *(Amphiprion melanopus)*
This fish, sometimes called the Dusky Anemone Fish, is a dull shade of brownish-fawn and is the least colorful species in the genus. It is really common only in Ceylonese waters. Its low price and hardiness recommend it to the marine aquarist who has gained some initial experience with damselfishes.

Pink Skunk Clownfish *(Amphiprion perideraion)*
The unfortunate common name of this attractive fish refers to the white stripe running along the dorsal median surface and not to its smell. It is most common in the central Pacific areas, although a very smilar species (again possibly only a geographical variation) named Yellow Skunk Clownfish *(A. akallopsis)* is common in the Indian Ocean (see page 8).

These clownfishes are more shy than other members of the genus; in the wild I have never seen them stray more than 8 to 12 inches from the anemone home base. For this reason, whenever possible skunk clownfishes should be kept in small groups of four to six in tanks containing no other fishes. Enough anemones should be provided to keep all the fishes happy. Whereas other clownfishes may do quite well without anemones in the tank, it would be cruel to keep skunk clownfishes under these conditions.

Maroon Clownfish *(Amphiprion [Premnas] biaculeatus)*
This species, sometimes called the Spine-cheeked Anemone Fish, is the aristocrat of the group both in ultimate size and coloration. Maroon Clownfishes are found in the Philippines area but are nowhere common and are usually the most expensive of the family to purchase. In their curious manner of swimming, body shape and anemone-loving habits they are similar to fishes of the genus *Amphiprion.* Yet, because of several important differences, the most obvious of which are the two curved knife-like appendages on the sides of the

116

Teak Clownfish

Pink Skunk Clownfish

Maroon Clownfish

head, they have been placed in the separate genus *Premnas*.

Aggression is not only noticeable between unmated members of the same species, but there appears to be a historic vendetta between the Maroon Clownfish and the Red Clownfish. It is either a reckless or a very skillful aquarist who has one of each coexisting in the same aquarium.

Saddleback Clownfish *(Amphiprion polymnus)*
Although it is not spectacularly colored, this species has the twin virtues of reaching a good size in captivity (up to 6 inches) and also of being generally well mannered. Most specimens that are offered for sale originate in the Philippines.

Wrasses (Family Labridae)
Cuban Hogfish *(Bodianus pulchellus)* and Spanish Hogfish *(B. rufus)*
On the reef, the Cuban Hogfish, also called the Spotfin Hogfish, and the Spanish Hogfish are usually found in deep waters (i.e., seldom less than 30 feet deep). However, it is amazing how quickly they adapt to the shallow depths of the home marine aquarium, settling down to become valued members of any collection. In coloration, the Cuban Hogfish is rare among diurnal coral fishes in that it is a glorious pink, with enamel-white and daffodil-yellow markings.

After several months in captivity, these fishes will eat anything they are offered, including dried flake foods. For the first two weeks under aquarium conditions, however, it may be necessary to offer food which more closely approaches the wild-state diet, for example strips of freshly sterilized mussel and squid flesh, prawn meat and prawn eggs.

In January 1968, I was in Cleveland, Ohio and stopped to visit the city's magnificent Public Aquarium. After discussing several problems with the aquarium director, he and the aquarium's chief diver drove me to Cleveland Airport. On the way we stopped off to see a marine dealer and my two colleagues made me a gift of a Cuban Hogfish and a Royal Gramma. The weather at the time was unbelievably cold and although the fishes were kept at cabin temperature on my transatlantic flight to England they suffered considerable exposure during the journey from the airport to my home. On arrival, I discovered their water to be at 58° F. The Royal Gramma had been dead for hours but the

Cuban Hogfish

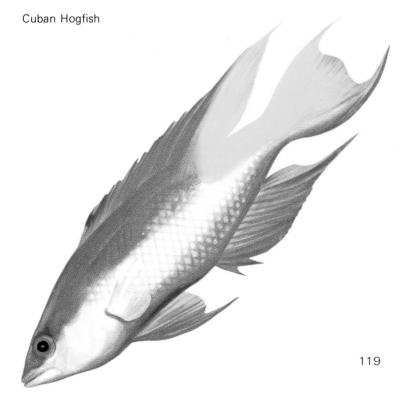

Spanish Hogfish

hogfish was still breathing very shallowly, although it was completely immobile. I left the fish in its original water to avoid needless additional chemical shock, and two hours later when the temperature had risen to 76° F, light aeration was introduced into its bag. The fish began to move around and half an hour later its water was gradually mixed with aquarium water and the fish released into the tank, where it spent the next year in perfect health.

Green Parrot Wrasse *(Thalassoma lunare)* and Chocolate Rainbow Wrasse *(T. purpureum)*

All the wrasses have a curious mode of swimming. The body is moved very little and the fish apparently propels itself along using only the pectoral fins. In the Green Parrot, or Moon, Wrasse, this curious gait, which causes the fish to 'hop' through the water, reaches its highest development. However, when frightened or if pursuing another fish, the wrasse will bring into action the swift lateral undulating movements of the body, resulting in short bursts of speed unequalled by any other coral-reef fish. Thus we have the paradoxical situation of a family of fishes whose movements are normally slow and clumsy but which, when

120

required, can produce unparalleled bursts of speed.

Anyone who has ever handled wrasses out of water will know that their mucous coating is exceptionally thick and slimy. In fact, the common name of one wrasse from the Caribbean is 'Slippery Dick'—a most apt name for the family as a whole. Therefore, when removing a wrasse from the water, great care must be taken if the fish is not, as a result of its own frightened behavior, to end up on the floor.

The Green Parrot Wrasse and its close relative the Chocolate Rainbow Wrasse both have undemanding appetites. When new in the aquarium, they may be slightly choosy with regard to diet, but once established and living in harmony with the other inhabitants of the tank, they quickly adapt to all foodstuffs. Most fishes in this group, if given a free choice, will select mostly animal protein such as mussel and scallop flesh, crab, prawn and shrimp meat, and so must be regarded as being essentially carnivorous in the wild state. However, they are so adaptable in captivity that few specimens will refuse a good-quality dried food when kept in good conditions.

Both species of the genus *Thalassoma* illustrated here have a very wide range extending from the East African coast in the west to the most eastern islands of the Pacific, but are absent from tropical Atlantic waters.

Green Parrot Wrasse

Cleaner Wrasse *(Labroides dimidiatus)*

This species, which is sometimes called the Blue Streak, must not be confused with the Neon Goby *(Elacatinus oceanops)*, which fulfills a very similar socioecological function in the tropical Atlantic. Throughout its enormous range in the Indo-Pacific, Pacific proper and Red Sea, this little wrasse is a very important fish. It removes parasites from all fishes on the reef. It is an astounding sight to see one of these tiny fishes swimming fearlessly into the mouth and gill-chamber of a 40-pound grouper that, if it so wished, could consume 50 or more at one sitting. The huge predator never attempts to eat his benefactor, however, although he may be seen to wince occasionally if the little 'doctor' is clumsy in his surgery. The great dependence that many coral-reef fishes must have on the Cleaner Wrasse was recently demonstrated by a field worker who removed all the Cleaner

Chocolate Rainbow Wrasse

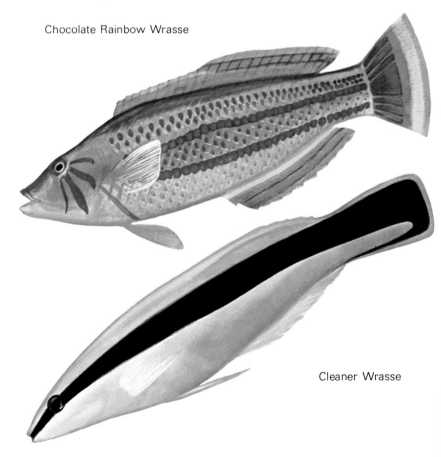

Cleaner Wrasse

Wrasses from a small area of the reef for a short period. The decline in both the variety and number of species in the area was considerable, and the missing population did not return until the Cleaner Wrasses were reinstated.

In the aquarium, the Cleaner Wrasse will ideally find an insufficient number of ectoparasites infecting the other fishes and will usually demonstrate its gastronomic versatility by eating normal aquarium foods. It is more than usually susceptible to changes in water quality, and seems not to favor unmatured synthetic sea water or any synthetic sea waters of poor formulation. Consequently, it is not advisable to introduce the fish into sea water that is less than one month old, and even then there must be a complete absence of nitrite. All possible precautions must be taken to prevent any kind of shock developing during and immediately after the introduction of this species to an aquarium.

Birdmouth Wrasse *(Gomphosus varius)*
The Birdmouth Wrasse, also known as the Hawaiian Birdfish, ranges from East Africa, up into the Red Sea and across the Pacific Ocean. It is distinguished by its magnifi-

Birdmouth Wrasse

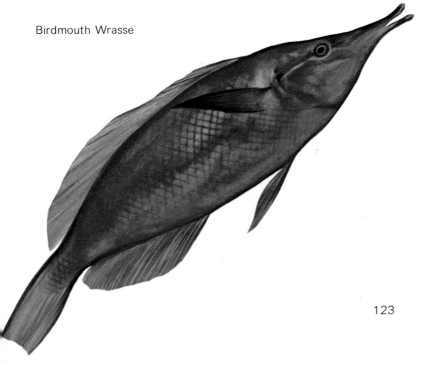

cent coloration of deep cobalt blue, with blue-green fins. Another feature that eliminates confusion with any other species is the elongation of the mouth into a beaklike structure. This fish is one of the hardiest in the family.

Clown Wrasse *(Coris gaimard)*

This fish has been referred to earlier with reference to the astonishing changes in coloration and patterning that take place as it matures (see page 5). The species *C. formosa* and *C. africana* of the Indo-Pacific and *C. gaimard* of the central and eastern Pacific may in fact be a single species that shows variation over a large geographical range. The most beautiful Clown Wrasses come from the Philippines. In these fishes the red parts of the body are especially vivid.

If inexpertly handled on introduction to an aquarium, all the wrasses can go into a state of shock: the animal lies on the bottom, often on its side as though dead and breathes rapidly. The beginner usually reaches for a stick and prods the hapless animal into activity. This has the reverse of the desired effect and often deepens the shock to a fatal level. Instead, the tank lights should be turned off, aeration and filtration turned to maximum, and the tank blackened out by

Clown Wrasse

covering it with thick cloth or paper. The aquarium should be left like this for a minimum of 12 hours. At the end of this period, after nightfall and with the room lights off, working perhaps with the aid of an assistant's flashlight, the aquarist should remove the covering from the aquarium. Leaving the curtains of the room open, he should now retire from the room. With the light of dawn the following day, the fish will usually be found eagerly searching for food, totally recovered and none the worse for its experience. The larger *Thalassoma*, *Coris* and *Gomphosus* species of wrasses will often react to introduction to an aquarium by diving into the gravel and will not emerge during daylight until assured of their safety in the new surroundings. Once settled in, the Clown Wrasse proves to be a hardy aquarium fish, eating all it is offered but showing a strong preference for fresh protein.

Twinspot Wrasse *(Coris angulata)*
This gorgeous animal is rarely offered for sale. However, in certain areas of East African reefs, it is a very common wrasse. It is difficult to collect because when approached to within 6 to 12 inches, it plummets straight into the sand.

Twinspot Wrasse

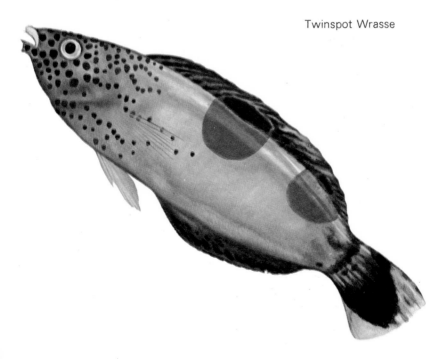

Dragonfishes (Family Scorpaenidae)
Common Dragonfish *(Pterois volitans)*
For the beginner uninterested in damselfishes and prepared to pay a little more, the Dragonfish (Lionfish or Turkeyfish) is an excellent alternative. It is very hardy, easy to feed and not aggressive to fishes too large for it to eat.

The Dragonfish on the reef is predatory, living on small fishes, but it will learn to eat suitably sized pieces of flesh in the aquarium. For the first ten days or so, it may be necessary to feed it on small, inexpensive freshwater fishes, such as female guppies, but after two days' starvation, a healthy Dragonfish will always accept a small piece of steak or prawn provided that it sees it falling through the water. The movement is important because the fish's feeding response is triggered off only by moving objects.

Dragonfish owners must be careful to avoid contact with the first 11 spines of the dorsal fin, as these contain a toxic venom. A colleague of mine was unlucky enough to run his hands on these dorsal spines. He immediately began to suffer shooting pains in the arm and eventually collapsed to his knees. A strong tourniquet was applied and the local ambulance service alerted. Fifteen minutes later the affected area was puffing up and the pain was excruciating, but on arrival at the hospital the victim was given injections and was soon making a speedy recovery. I tell this story not to deter anyone from buying one of the several attractive *Pterois* species but to caution the prospective owner. These fishes use their venomous spines only as defensive deterrents and never as offensive weapons. However, the dangers of allowing a child to own one will be self-evident. The Common Dragonfish has a circumtropical range, with the exclusion of the tropical Atlantic area.

Regal Dragonfish *(Pterois radiata)*
This exotic-looking creature is just as potentially dangerous as the Common Dragonfish. All comments regarding the Common Dragonfish apply to this species, the only differences being that *P. radiata* is slightly more delicate in captivity and not as easy to wean onto a meat diet.

Common Dragonfish (*top*) and Regal Dragonfish (*bottom*)

127

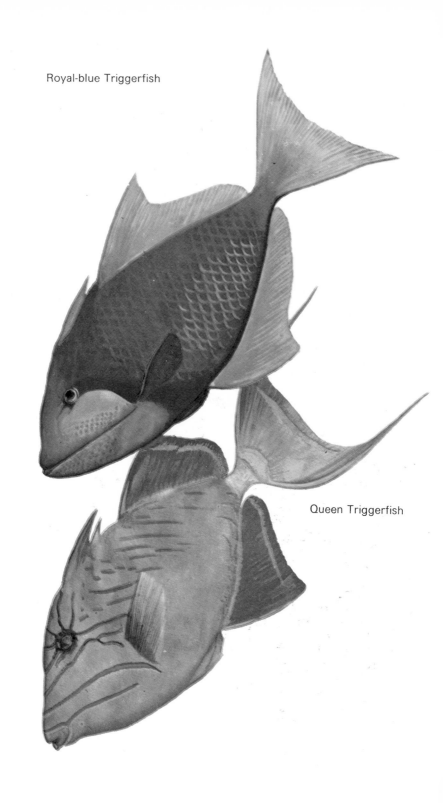

Royal-blue Triggerfish

Queen Triggerfish

Triggerfishes (Family Balistidae)
Royal-blue Triggerfish *(Odonus niger)*

This family is characterized by two traits—extreme hardiness and an aggressive nature. Provided that due allowance is made for the latter characteristic, many of the family are suitable for beginners. Generally, the Royal-blue, or Redfang, Triggerfish is the least aggressive, although individuals may differ greatly in this respect.

The common name 'triggerfish' probably arose because of a curious modification of the dorsal fin into a stiff spike that can be erected at will and then locked or 'triggered' into place. If the fish has swum into a small coral crevice and erected its dorsal and often a similar ventral spike, the collector finds it almost impossible to remove the fish from its lair, so firmly is it wedged into place. The Royal-blue Triggerfish is most common around Ceylon, but it does extend in diminishing numbers to the far-eastern coral islands of the Pacific.

The triggerfishes appear to be sensitive to a high concentration of aluminum salts in the water. Respiration is seriously affected and they begin to secrete copious amounts of grayish-white mucus. Death usually follows within a few hours unless the fishes are quickly removed to sea water with a normal aluminum concentration.

Feeding triggerfishes seldom presents any major problems. In the wild their chosen foods seem to be mostly crustaceans, such as small crabs, prawns, shrimps, lobsters and mollusks. Their massive and powerful jaws are ideally adapted for crushing.

Queen Triggerfish *(Balistes vetula)*

This beautiful species is marred as an aquarium fish by its very belligerent nature, although the persistent aquarist may occasionally spot relatively peaceful specimens. There are reports that this species is occasionally found off the southeastern coast of Africa, but it is really common only in the Caribbean area.

Black Triggerfish *(Xanichthys ringens)*

This is one of the few truly circumtropical species kept in the home marine aquarium. The Black Triggerfish is almost

Black Triggerfish

Clown Triggerfish

as common in the tropical Atlantic as it is in the Indo-Pacific. It is one of the less aggressive triggerfishes and may be kept with most show fishes that are as large as, or preferably larger than, the specimen. A typical community in, for example, an 80-gallon aquarium would be: one Black Triggerfish, one large angelfish (either a Koran, Emperor, Purple Moon or Bluering Angelfish), one large Common Dragonfish, one small, 24-inch moray eel and one large wrasse (either a Twinspot or Green Parrot Wrasse). To establish such a community as peacefully as possible, it would be wise to settle the other species in together for two to three weeks before adding the Black Triggerfish.

Clown Triggerfish *(Balistoides niger)*
When this magnificent creature is exhibited, it is often proclaimed as 'the most expensive fish in the world'. Whereas this may have been true a few years ago, one can now buy a large specimen for almost half the cost of a Majestic Angelfish because of a curious anomaly in the pricing structure of Clown Triggerfishes. The normal rule is 'small fish—low cost, large fish—high cost'. However, this is reversed in the Clown Triggerfishes because they spawn in relatively deep water where the young remain until they attain a length of 6 to 8 inches. It is only when they have reached this size that they occasionally wander onto the reef for food, where they can be captured by divers. Hence, small specimens are at a premium and command very high prices.

Variations in triggerfish behavior reach a peak in this species. Occasional specimens are more ferocious than piranhas. I carry a long scar on my right wrist from a previously mild-mannered 8-inch Clown Triggerfish that attacked savagely one day as I rearranged the rockwork in its tank. Most specimens, except in very large tanks, are not to be trusted with any other fishes.

Jigsaw Triggerfish *(Pseudobalistes fuscus)*
This oddly marked fish appears to be limited to the Indian Ocean and the western Indo-Pacific area, as it is never listed by any of the Hawaiian, Japanese or Filipino collectors. Most specimens come from the area around Ceylon.

131

The Jigsaw Triggerfish does not show the extremes of behavioral instability found in the Clown Triggerfish. This is to say that one seldom finds a truly docile Jigsaw Triggerfish, but equally rarely finds a violently aggressive specimen. Provided a marine aquarium of more than 100 gallons is available with plenty of rocky caves and crevices, this species may be uneventfully kept with other large show fishes. It would, however, be wise not to include any other triggerfishes in the collection, whatever the size of the aquarium. [This rule also applies to all large show fishes except schooling species such as Yellow Jacks *(Caranx speciosus)* or Striped Catfishes *(Plotosus anguillaris)*.]

Yellow-striped Emerald Triggerfish *(Balistapus undulatus)*

This attractively marked but very aggressive triggerfish, sometimes called the Orange-striped or Red-lined Triggerfish, is circumtropical in distribution except for the tropical Atlantic regions. It is exceptionally tough and disease-free in the marine aquarium but should not be trusted with any except the largest show fishes, even in a very large aquarium. The life-span in captivity, like all the triggerfishes, is very long; it is not uncommon for a healthy specimen to live for 6 to 7 years if obtained at a juvenile 2 to 3 inches. Feeding is trouble-free, provided that plenty of fresh protein is available.

Picasso Triggerfish (Rhinecanthus aculeatus)

The Picasso Triggerfish is so named because of the 'abstract' designs on its flanks. However, it is also known as the 'Humuhumu-nukunuku-a-puaa' Triggerfish in the Hawaiian chain. It is often obtainable at a length of 1 to 2 inches, making it a great favorite because at this size the young fishes are not particularly aggressive.

Filefishes (Family Monocanthidae)
Orange-emerald Filefish *(Oxymonocanthus longirostris)* and Fantailed Filefish *(Pervagor spilosoma)*

According to one of my more reliable overseas collectors, these filefishes reach almost 24 inches in length in the wild,

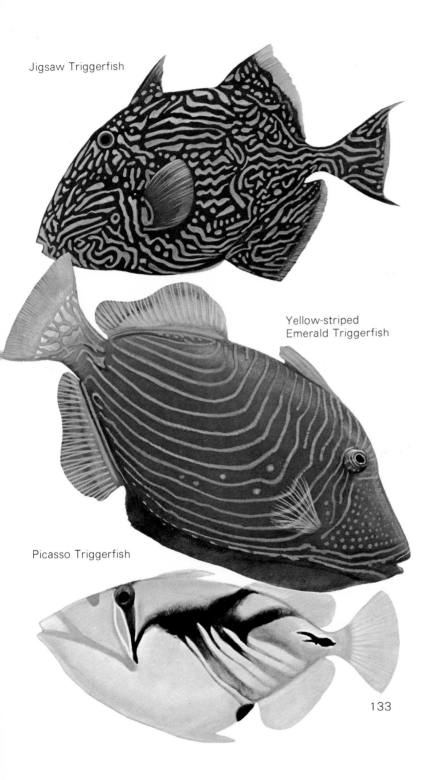

Jigsaw Triggerfish

Yellow-striped
Emerald Triggerfish

Picasso Triggerfish

133

although they are rarely seen elsewhere longer than 2 to 3 inches. The Orange-emerald Filefish is also known as the Orange-spotted Filefish and in Australia as the Beaked Leatherjacket.

Filefishes are closely related to the triggerfishes and have the same dorsal and ventral spikes for security in their coral retreats, but in behavior and personality they differ greatly. Filefishes are the very essence of pacifism, even toward members of their own species, and they may be confidently bought by the less-experienced marine aquarist, who will have little difficulty in getting them to feed.

Filefishes can, however, be somewhat choosy about foods. On the coral reef they spend the majority of their time pecking at small coral polyps and sponges, and picking tiny crustaceans, mollusks and polyps from rocks and dead coral. In the home aquarium, they seem to ʾ best in small groups

Orange-emerald Filefish

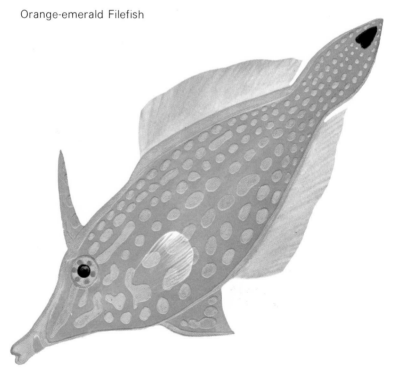

Fantailed Filefish

of two or three of their own species and will always begin feeding on newly hatched brine shrimp. After a week or two on this diet, they can be induced to change to vitamin-soaked, freeze-dried brine shrimp and later on to prawn eggs and finely chopped squid flesh. From then on, feeding presents no problem, and within a few days a good specimen will begin eating even a high-quality dried flake food.

Filefishes, more than triggerfishes, seem to appreciate a feeding of newly thawed frozen spinach two or three times a week. However, it is well to remember that this excellent food begins to decompose very quickly once thawed out and may cause severe internal disorders if eaten in a partially rotten state by a hungry fish. Therefore it must always be kept frozen in a refrigerator freezing compartment and a small piece broken off ten minutes before feeding time. This can then be thawed and immediately fed to the fishes.

Tetrasoma gibbosus

Trunkfishes (Family Ostraciontidae)

Tetrasoma gibbosus

This fish is a great favorite, possibly because of its whimsical appearance and appealing eyes. It has sometimes been called the 'Hovercraft' because its nearly transparent, rapidly beating pectoral fins make it seem to move through the water with no visible means of propulsion. Furthermore, in general shape, with the high, domed back and almost flat ventral surface, it somewhat resembles a hovercraft.

These fishes, also known as box-fishes, are found throughout the Indo-Pacific area but are never common and always command a good price when available. A good-sized adult specimen will reach almost 10 inches in length; at that time its general proportions resemble those of a small football with the bottom removed. However, most specimens suitable for the home marine aquarium are tennis ball size or smaller and make endearing pets, quickly becoming tame and learning to recognize their owner. I had one specimen so tame that it would swim onto a hand (submerged palm uppermost just under the surface) and allow itself to be lifted completely out of the water for a few seconds. This behavior shows the extraordinary trust coral-reef fishes can develop—to a degree not paralleled among freshwater fishes. For any fishes other than mudskippers, lungfishes, eels and a few others, such an action represents completely abnormal behavior requiring enormous faith and adaptability. No difficulty is experienced in feeding this species, all foods being eagerly accepted.

Longhorn Cowfish *(Lactoria cornuta)*
These 'armor-plated' boxfishes from the tropical Indo-Pacific are excellent community fishes. They are easy to feed and strongly resistant to most diseases.

Ostracion lentiginosus
These boxfishes, although beautifully marked, should be treated with great caution when introduced into an already established aquarium. If the water is not clean or if they are attacked and scared by the existing members of the tank, they react by producing a highly toxic, frothy substance around the mouth. This foam not only proves fatal for the offending attacker but also for all the fishes in the aquarium, including *Ostracion lentiginosum.*

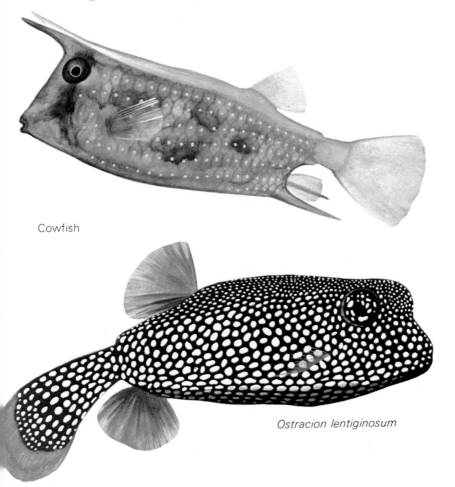

Cowfish

Ostracion lentiginosum

Porcupine fishes (Family Diodontidae)
Common Porcupine fish *(Diodon hystrix)*
There are many fishes similar in appearance in the genus *Diodon,* and most are offered for sale from time to time indiscriminately labeled as *'Diodon hystrix'*. However, there is very little variation among the species with regard to their needs and behavior.

The Porcupine fish, like the pufferfishes, is distinguished by its ability to swallow huge amounts of water, inflating itself to many times its original size. Inflated, it looks like a football with the face of a Pekinese dog and the tail of a fish. Occasionally, when badly panicked, the Porcupine fish makes the mistake of coming to the surface and inflating itself with air. Whereas most specimens can release this air when the source of provocation is removed, a few seem to have a defective release mechanism, and consequently float around on the surface, dehydrating until they perish.

When in the inflated state, the spines covering the body stand out at an angle. It is believed that by inflating itself the large spiky fish looks less attractive to a predator. It will be apparent to most people, therefore, that since this self-inflating ability is only used as a response to fright, it is extremely cruel to continually terrify a captive Porcupine fish in order to demonstrate the phenomenon.

Common Porcupine fish

The porcupine fishes are easy to feed on any kind of proteinaceous matter such as earthworm, squid, mussel, steak, heart and washed, chopped liver.

Pufferfishes (Family Canthigasteridae)

Diamond-flecked Pufferfish *(Canthigaster solandri)*

This animal is very common throughout the central and Indo-Pacific. It is hardy and resistant to disease and consequently easily shipped—a combination of circumstances producing a fish that is always readily available at low prices. This species will eat any kind of flesh, once acclimatized to aquarium life.

Minstrel Pufferfish *(Canthigaster valentini)*

The comments for the previous species apply to the Minstrel Pufferfish although it is more rare in the wild. In common with the Diamond-flecked Pufferfish, it is able to make an angry grunting noise when upset.

Diamond-flecked Pufferfish

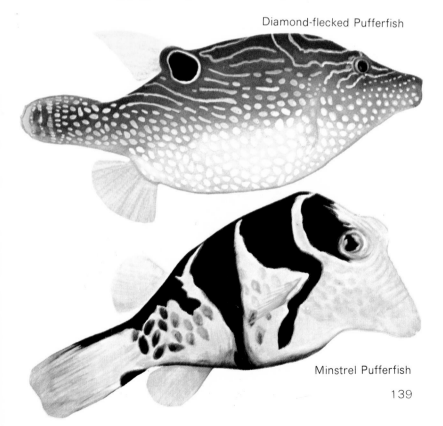

Minstrel Pufferfish

Stoichactis anemone

Fanworm

Live coral head of *Goniopora*

140

INVERTEBRATES FOR THE AQUARIUM

Coelenterates

These animals are characterized by a hollow tubular body, usually closed at one end (the foot) with an opening at the other (the mouth), fringed with tentacles. Two groups suitable for the home marine aquarium are anemones and corals.

Anemones

Generally the hardiest anemones are the genus *Stoichactis*. These animals vary in size from a mouth disc as little as 2 inches across to specimens several feet in diameter. To keep the larger anemones, large tank, of a minimum size of 72 inches x 24 inches x 18 inches is required.

Anemones are very susceptible to sudden changes in water quality and, when introducing one to the aquarium, at least an hour should be taken in slowing mixing the waters together. Their vitamin requirements, particularly of B_{12} and B_1, appear to be quite high, and a good vitamin concentrate should be added to the small pieces of meat they are fed every other day or so. When buying an anemone, check that all the tentacles and the oral disc are fully extended and look healthy. If any part is collapsed or appears to be breaking up, the specimen should be rejected.

Anemones of the genus *Discosoma* have an oral disc covered with thousands of minute, densely packed tentacles, giving an impression of coarse velvet. They are not as tough as the *Stoichactis* species and are only suitable for the advanced marine aquarist.

Living corals

These tiny colonial animals, individually called polyps, are best suited for the natural-system aquarium, representing one of the few natural methods of mechanical filtration. The polyp has the same coelenterate body plan but on a much smaller scale than the anemone, and it extracts calcium and magnesium salts from the water, thus building up a hard, limey tube around itself. Corals and the larger fan-worms or tubeworms are filter feeders, continually removing planktonic organisms from the water.

141

Echinoderms
All the echinoderms (spiny-skinned animals) exhibit a common body design (i.e., they are radially symmetrical). This means there is no bilateral symmetry (no right- and left-hand side) as in the higher animals such as mammals and birds. Instead, there is symmetry in form in a plane at right angles to the central axis. The echinoderms commonly seen in the marine aquarium are the starfishes and sea urchins.

Starfishes
Almost all the starfishes kept in tropical marine aquaria appear to be filter feeders (i.e., they will not accept pieces of meat). Consequently they should be kept only in semi-natural or natural marine tanks, as they would slowly starve to death in a clinical-system aquarium.

Sea urchins
These invertebrates and particularly the Black Sea Urchins do very well in the marine aquarium on a diet of prawn, steak and earthworm. They appear to be omnivorous in the wild and in the aquarium relish a piece of lettuce or spinach twice a week. All foods for the sea urchin should be dropped into the spines. These spines will then slowly maneuver the food down and around to the mouth (Aristotle's lantern), located in the center of the ventral surface of the animal.

Mollusks
The mollusks which are best for the marine aquarium are, in order of hardiness, cowries, conches, clams, nudibranchs and flame scallops. The cowries, in which the mantle occasionally flows completely around the shell hiding it from view, are very hardy in old, established seminatural- or natural-system aquaria. Most species will graze continually on the algae that coat all surfaces within the aquarium, although they should be occasionally offered small pieces of finely chopped meat. These comments also apply to the conches, which move around the tank with a cumbersome, but amusing, hopping motion. The beautiful shell-less nudibranchs graze on sessile planktonic organisms, while both the clams and flame scallops are filter feeders.

142

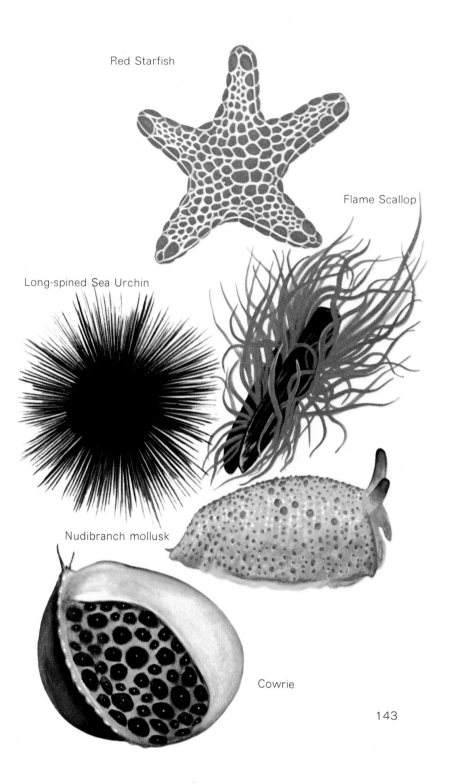

Red Starfish

Flame Scallop

Long-spined Sea Urchin

Nudibranch mollusk

Cowrie

143

Octopus (Octopus)

The octopus is a member of the molluscan class Cephalopoda, which also includes the cuttlefishes and squids. In these highly developed invertebrates there is a tendency for the shell to become vestigial, with a corresponding increase in activity, maneuverability and ferocity. An amazingly complex nervous and sensory system has developed, as well as the predatory habits that usually go with them. The eye of the octopus has developed to such an extent that it rivals even that of the mammals in efficiency. The foot of the octopus has developed into a circle of arms around the mouth well equipped with a pair of horny parrotlike jaws capable of giving a nasty bite.

A small specimen between 18 and 30 inches in length can make a fascinating subject for study. Feeding is easy to achieve, provided that the animal's territorial requirement is catered to. The aquarium should be as large as possible and contain many nooks and crannies, crevices, caves and shelves. With an animal as nervous and psychologically complicated as the octopus, detailed attention to the design of the aquarium decor is as vital as attention to the water quality.

Having created a suitably complicated and reassuringly natural habitat for the octopus, the tank should be filled with the best-quality synthetic sea water available. Several days should be allowed under full filtration and aeration for the water to mature. For gravel to cover the undergravel filter use old 'ripe' gravel that has been lightly washed in clean, warm sea water (Never wash matured gravel with fresh water for this will destroy the nitrifying bacteria coating every particle. Never throw matured marine aquarium gravel away—it is precious).

The octopus should be introduced into the aquarium very slowly, taking perhaps 35 to 45 minutes, in almost total darkness. When the waters have been gradually mixed, the octopus, if it has not already done so, may be encouraged to climb out of the plastic bag into its new home. Feeding should be attempted the following day with small pieces of prawn, shrimp or crab flesh. Although most species of octopus are nocturnal feeders, they are such gluttonous animals that they can be easily encouraged to feed and disport themselves during daylight hours.

It is almost impossible to keep fishes with an octopus since they are nearly always caught and eaten by the octopus within a few days. However, a well-fed octopus will not usually interfere with live corals, tubeworms, starfishes, sea urchins or anemones.

Octopus

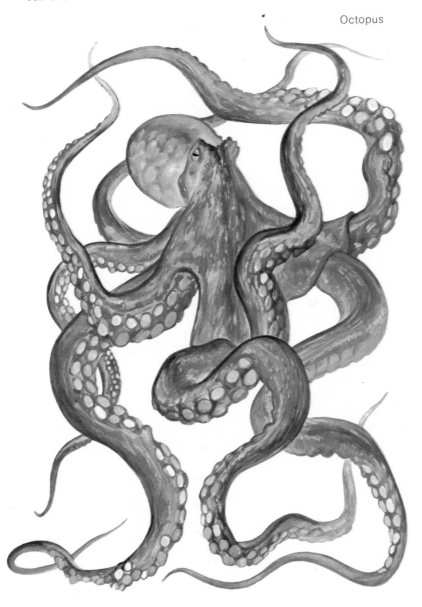

Crustaceans

The crustaceans include the crabs, prawns, shrimps, lobsters and crayfishes. Many are exceptionally hardy and ideal for the beginner's marine invertebrate aquarium.

Boxing Shrimp *(Stenopus hispidus)*

This spectacular little crustacean does very well in the marine aquarium provided that it is regularly fed. Many people buy these animals as scavengers and then, because they have a new aquarium with 'unripened' gravel (lacking a population of nitrifying bacteria), embark on a program of sparse feeding, forgetting all about *Stenopus,* waiting on the bottom of the tank for food that never falls down to it. The answer to this problem is either to feed the animals individually with tiny pieces of meat impaled on the end of a plastic knitting needle, or to withhold the purchase of Boxing Shrimps until such time as the gravel has completely matured bacteriologically (up to three months).

The ferocity of Boxing Shrimps to each other (except during the mating period) is startling. In view of this intraspecific aggression, which invariably ends in the death of one if not both of the combatants, it is extremely cruel to house more than one shrimp in a tank smaller than 150 gallons.

Mantis shrimps

These animals are responsible for those tiny pyramids of sand often seen on the sea bed in the tropics. In the aquarium they rarely prove to be hardy animals, and only very advanced marine aquarists should consider attempts at culturing the species.

Hermit crabs

These are crustaceans in which the normal protective chitinous exoskeleton is absent on the abdomen. To protect its vulnerable parts from predators, the hermit crab adopts an empty shell of a univalve mollusk (for example a whelk) into which it can safely tuck its abdomen. When the animal grows too large for the shell, it discards it and adopts a new, larger one. In the marine aquarium, hermit crabs are very interesting and hardy scavengers.

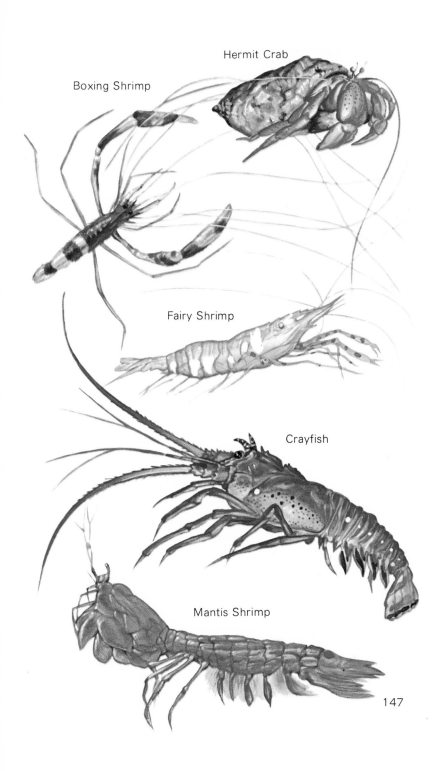

Boxing Shrimp

Hermit Crab

Fairy Shrimp

Crayfish

Mantis Shrimp

Marine live food

Examples: shrimps, prawns, sandhoppers, crab and lobster flesh and the liver, mantle and foot of freshly killed mussels

ADVANTAGES
May well provide vital trace elements. Usually stays alive in the tank if not eaten immediately.

DISADVANTAGES
Unless properly quarantined, marine live food may well transmit diseases to aquarium fishes. It is difficult to keep alive in store.

FEEDING AQUARIUM ANIMALS

Feeding and water management are probably the two most difficult aspects of marine aquarium keeping for the beginner to master. Whereas there are certain clearly laid down steps for establishing a marine tank for either the natural, semi-natural or clinical systems, so much of what separates a good 'feeder' and good 'manager' from their less fortunate alternatives, is attributable to experience, common sense and that most intangible quality, 'salty-fingers'.

The general rule that should always be adhered to is 'a little food often'. This principle is most vitally important during the critical first three months, during which time the *nitrifying potential* of the aquarium (the ability of the bacteria in the gravel to oxidize waste matter to harmless nitrates) is steadily increasing but not at a high enough level to tolerate careless over-feeding. Throughout the whole of this period, unless de-ionizing resins are being used in a power filter, the water will have a low and constantly diminishing nitrite reading. This is one of the many reasons why the beginner is urged to keep damselfishes for the first three

Other live food

Examples: earthworms, whiteworms, grindal worms, *Daphia, Tubifex,* mosquito larvae, young livebearers (mollies, guppies, platies, swordtails)

ADVANTAGES

Cannot carry diseases to aquarium fishes and is fairly easy to keep alive in store. This live food can be readily obtained.

DISADVANTAGES

Some fishes will not take to these foods initially and will require patient weaning before they will feed readily.

Comparison of the advantages and disadvantages of marine and other live aquarium food.

months or, if he prefers larger fishes, snappers, triggerfishes, dragonfishes or the batfish *Platax orbicularis.*

It is a good idea to get into the habit of determining when an animal is in a feeding mood. The signs to watch for are alertness of eye movement which in the case of butterfly fishes and angelfishes shows itself as a series of active, close-range examinations of pieces of coral and rockwork, with occasional pecking at real or imagined objects thereon. The more active or predatory animals such as snappers, triggerfishes, dragonfishes, wrasses and Nurse Sharks will often show their hunger by chasing up and down the aquarium in a generally alert fashion.

The next precaution to take is that the correct type of food is offered to the fishes in correct-sized particles. For example, it would be ridiculous to offer spinach to a dragonfish and as foolish to offer a single prawn egg to a 9-inch Emperor Snapper, or a half-inch cube of prawn flesh to a butterfly fish.

149

DISEASES OF FISHES

Oodinium

The most important and only really common disease of tropical marine fishes is caused by the protozoan dinoflagellate *Oodinium ocellatum*. It is particularly virulent in its attacks upon juvenile fishes—especially in an overcrowded aquarium. It is a swift killer unless promptly treated with one of several available brands of medication (e.g., 'Cuprazin'). The parasite cannot normally be seen on the body until the disease is advanced and often incurable. Even then the grayish-white to fawn-yellow cysts are so small that they are unlikely to be seen unless the fish is viewed head on with rear lighting. The parasites attack primarily the gill filaments, and it is not until they have weakened the fish by partial asphyxiation that they can establish themselves on the body. The best indication of an incipient *Oodinium* infection is a sudden increase in the respiratory rate (shown by the number of movements made by the gill covers). A normal rate for a healthy fish is 80 to 110 gill movements per minute. It must be remembered that factors other than *Oodinium* infection can affect the respiratory rate, but if the pH, specific gravity, temperature, nitrite and ammonia levels are all within normal limits and yet the breathing rate is increased, it is safe to assume that the fishes are suffering from an *Oodinium* infection.

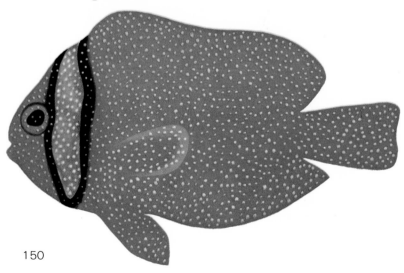

Possibly *Oodinium* disease is latent in all marine fishes and only develops under physical, chemical or psychological stress. Aquarists are strongly advised to treat all new fishes with a good *Oodinium* cure as soon as they are settled into their aquarium.

Lymphocystis

This disease is most common among Caribbean fishes kept in water that has previously contained Indo-Pacific fishes. However, any marine fishes can be infected by *Lymphocystis* and, because it is a viral infection, no known medication is effective against it, not even antibiotics. However, one need not destroy fishes suffering from *Lymphocystis* as is sometimes recommended. Provided that the cysts are cleanly cut away and the cut areas are sterilized by a light brushing of one percent acriflavine solution, an otherwise healthy fish will make a rapid recovery.

Fishes suffering from *Oodinium* disease (*opposite*) and *Lymphocystis* (*below*)

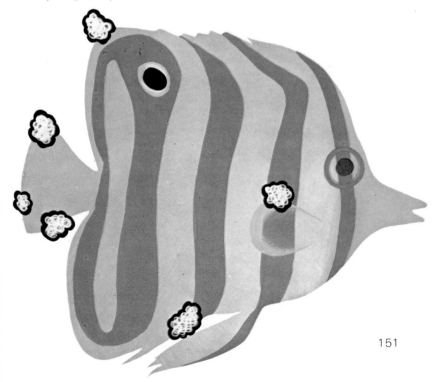

White-spot disease
This is caused by a protozoan parasite of the genus *Ichthy-ophthirius* that embeds itself in the skin and produces grayish-white hemispherical cysts about one-fourth the size of a pinhead. It is less dangerous but more difficult to cure than *Oodinium* and is treated in the same way.

Benedenia
Large, gray-white, triangular flukes fix onto the body with the apex toward the tail. Large angelfishes subjected to a high nitrite level often succumb to this disease. It is easily cured using a good *Oodinium* cure and is one of the easiest diseases to detect.

Ichthyophonus fungus
This attacks the internal organs, and there is as yet no practical cure. It is extremely rare among coral-reef fishes. Infection usually takes the form of the fish developing a ravenous appetite but losing weight rapidly. I have had limited success in prolonging the life of the fishes with daily injections of streptomycin, penicillin and vitamin B_{12} for five days. This is a widely distributed species of fungus.

Saprolegnia fungi
These occasionally attack marine fishes. The disease is cured almost in hours by bubbling ozonized air into the water. An aquarist without an ozonizer should not buy young Koran Angels, which commonly suffer from this disease.

Finrot and bodyrot
These loose terms cover the effect of several types of pathogenic bacteria on coral-reef fishes. If the quality of the water is good and the animals are not deficient in any vitamins, such attacks are very rare. If the water is occasionally ozonized, they are virtually nonexistent. As ozonizers are still expensive, it should be stated that an effective cure is to apply a bactericidal solution such as acriflavine, proflavine, mercurochrome or a solution of one teaspoonful of 16 vols. hydrogen peroxide solution in an eggcupful of water. Avoid contact of the hydrogen peroxide with eyes or gills.

White spot

Benedenia

Finrot and bodyrot

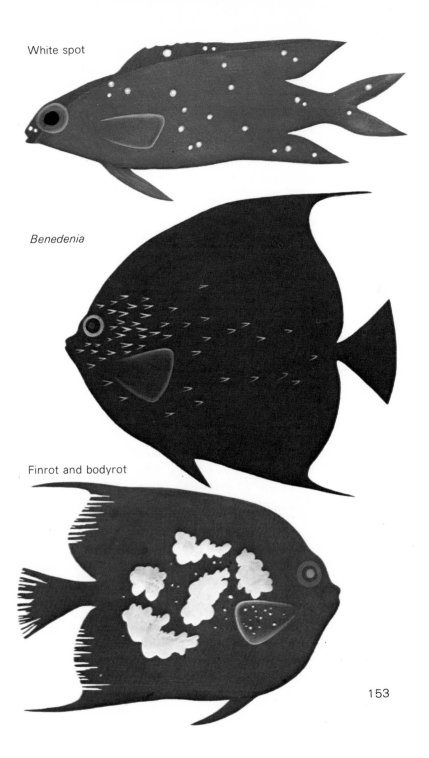

GENERAL HINTS FOR THE BEGINNER

Never	overfeed your fishes. Always keep your tank as clean as possible by removing any un-eaten food, and introduce as much variety as possible into the diet.
Never	overcrowd the aquarium. It is better to have a few fishes in radiant health than many gulping fishes, battle-scarred through fighting over inadequate territory.
Never	open a traveling box containing marine fishes in strong light, and always make the transition from plastic bag to aquarium as gradually as possible.
Never	add small fishes to an aquarium that already contains large and well-established fishes, unless you have expert knowledge of the natures of both the resident fishes and the new addition.
Never	remove invertebrate animals from the water when transferring them from aquarium to aquarium. They should be placed in a water-filled plastic bag held underwater and

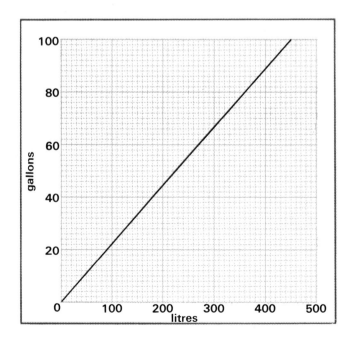

released in the same fashion. This will prevent pockets of air being trapped in their bodies which they may not be able to get rid of.

Never use lead to weight down a floating object. Lead and the traces of zinc which it often contains, as well as copper, brass, bronze and aluminum, are all toxic in excess to marine life. It is safer to use a piece of silicone rubber, nylon or a nontoxic plastic to weight a piece of coral or rock.

Always check regularly the specific gravity, temperature and pH of your water.

Always be aware of the following early indications of fouling in sea water: frothing at the water surface; water becoming cloudy; fishes breathing more rapidly than normal (could also be disease); water producing fetid odor.

Always provide as much coral and rockwork as possible for shy species.

Always check all fishes are present at feeding time.

Always ensure that all corals, shells, gorgonian and sea-fan skeletons are thoroughly cured (and that no trace of chlorine odor clings to them) before using them inside the marine aquarium.

Aquarium volume (*opposite*) and temperature (*below*) conversion graphs

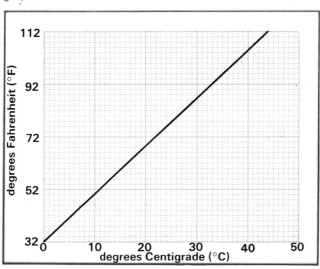

BOOKS TO READ

The following books are recommended for further general reading and are usually available from bookstores and public libraries.

Know How to Keep Saltwater Fishes by W. Braker. The Pet Library, 1968.

Enjoy a Saltwater Aquarium by W. Braker. The Pet Library, 1968.

Caribbean Reef Fishes by J. C. Randall. T.F.H. Publications, 1968.

Salt-Water Aquarium Fish by H. R. Axelrod and W. Vorderwinkler. T.F.H. Publications, 1965.

The Marine Aquarium by W. Wickler. Studio Vista. London, 1967.

Fishes of South Africa by J. B. L. Smith. Central News Agency Limited. South Africa, 1965 (fifth edition).

Tropical Fishes of the Great Barrier Reef by T. C. Marshall. Angus and Robertson. Sydney, 1967.

All About Tropical Fishes by D. McInerny and G. Gerard. Macmillan, 1958.

The Underwater Guide to Marine Life by C. Ray and E. Ciampi. Barnes, 1956.

The Captive Sea by C. Phillips. Chilton Books, 1964.

Tropical Freshwater Aquaria by George Cust and Peter Bird. A Grosset All-Color Guide. Grosset & Dunlap, 1971.

Fishes of the World by Allan Cooper. A Grosset All-Color Guide. Grosset & Dunlap, 1971.

PLACES TO VISIT

New York Aquarium, Brooklyn, New York
Shedd Aquarium, Chicago, Illinois
Marineland, San Diego, California
Steinhart Aquarium, San Francisco, California
Cleveland Aquarium, Cleveland, Ohio
Municipal Aquarium, Key West, Florida

INDEX

KEY TO ALTERNATE COMMON NAMES

Common names used for given species vary greatly from place to place. Many alternates are given in the text and others are offered here to aid in identification.

NAME IN THIS VOLUME	ALTERNATES
Malayan Angel, p. 55	Mono; Fingerfish
Cerise Grouper, p. 60	Painted Coral Bass (or Grouper)
Wreckfish, p. 63	Pink Anthias; Lyretail Coralfish
Checkered Angelfish, p. 76	Ceylonese Angelfish
Majestic Angelfish, p. 76	Blue-girdled Angelfish
Wimplefish, p. 82	Heniochus; Bannerfish; Pennant-fish
Golden Butterfly Fish, p. 83	Filament Butterfly Fish
Sunburst Butterfly Fish, p. 86	Klein's Butterfly Fish
Rainbow Butterfly Fish, p. 88	Three-striped Butterfly Fish; Redfin Butterfly Fish
Emperor Tang, p. 92	Purple Tang; Yellowtail Tang
Majestic Surgeonfish, p. 95	Zebra Surgeonfish; Red Sea Surgeonfish
Regal Tang, p. 95	Flagtail Tang; Hippo Tang
Japanese Tang, p. 97	Lipstick Tang; Smooth-head Unicornfish
Rabbitfish, p. 101	Foxface
Arabian Snapper, p. 101	Blue-lined Snapper
Polka-dot Grunt, p. 103	Clown Sweetlips
Spotted Sweetlips, p. 103	Oriental Sweetlips
Green Forktail Damselfish, p. 104	Blue Chromis
Humbug Damselfish, p. 107	Banded Damselfish; Three-banded Damselfish; White-tailed Damselfish
Cloudy Damselfish, p. 108	Reticulated Damselfish
Electric-blue Damselfish, p. 111	Blue Devil
Regal Dragonfish, p. 126	Whitefin Lionfish
Royal-blue Triggerfish, p. 129	Redtooth Triggerfish; Black Triggerfish;
Black Triggerfish, p. 129	Blackfin Triggerfish; Sargassum Triggerfish
Jigsaw Triggerfish, p. 131	Blue-lined Triggerfish
Yellow-striped Emerald Trigger-fish, p. 132	Orange-striped Triggerfish; Yellow-striped Triggerfish
Orange-emerald Filefish, p. 132	Longnosed Filefish; Orange-spotted Filefish
Tetrasoma Gibbosus, p. 136	Thornback Trunkfish; Thornback Boxfish
Minstrel Pufferfish, p. 139	Saddleback Pufferfish; Sharpnose Pufferfish
Boxing Shrimp, p. 146	Banded Coral Shrimp